T0231946

Code Simplicity

Max Kanat-Alexander

O'REILLY®

Beijing · Cambridge · Farnham · Köln · Sebastopol · Tokyo

Code Simplicity
by Max Kanat-Alexander

Copyright © 2012 Max Kanat-Alexander. All rights reserved.
Printed in the United States of America.

Published by O'Reilly Media, Inc., 1005 Gravenstein Highway North, Sebastopol, CA 95472.

O'Reilly books may be purchased for educational, business, or sales promotional use. Online editions
are also available for most titles (*http://my.safaribooksonline.com*). For more information, contact our
corporate/institutional sales department: (800) 998-9938 or *corporate@oreilly.com*.

Editors: Andy Oram and Mike Hendrickson
Production Editor: Melanie Yarbrough
Copyeditor: Rachel Head

Cover Designer: Karen Montgomery
Interior Designer: David Futato
Illustrator: Robert Romano

Revision History for the First Edition:
　2012-03-22　　First release
　2012-06-13　　Second release
See *http://oreilly.com/catalog/errata.csp?isbn=9781449313890* for release details.

ISBN: 978-1-449-31389-0

[LSI]

1339264531

Table of Contents

Preface

Many years ago, I was given a unique opportunity. I started doing volunteer software development for an open-source project called "Bugzilla" that had famously messy code. It had reached what is usually considered the "point of no return" in software development—due to the complexity of the system, it was so hard to modify that all new feature work had slowed to a crawl. Most of the developers were throwing their hands up in the air and walking away from the project in frustration. After all, they were volunteers—they didn't have to deal with bad code if they didn't want to.

However, Bugzilla had been around for six years at that point, and it had millions of users. It was one of the backbones of open-source development on the Web—nearly every major open-source project was using it to keep track of the bugs they needed to fix in their software. Some companies—like Mozilla, the makers of Firefox—were using Bugzilla to keep track of every single task that every employee in the company was doing. If Bugzilla died as a project, it would have been a severe blow to the world of open-source development and in a smaller way, to the software industry as a whole.

So obviously, it had to survive. But how could we possibly do that? Normally at this point in the software development lifecycle, organizations tend to re-write their software. But due to developer attrition, we didn't have the resources to re-write. We barely had the resources to maintain the existing code!

So partially born out of necessity, but even more so out of an idealism that abhors throwing away an entire system just to re-write an identical one, I took on a crusade to fix up Bugzilla's existing code instead of re-writing it. I and a small group of new developers on the project re-architected the existing system piece by piece and shipped slightly improved new versions every few months. We were still writing new features while we did this, but always in a way that made the code better, not messier.

And it worked. Boy did it work. After three years of fixing up the code this way, we were pumping out features at twice the rate we used to with 1/4th the developers the project used to have (before they all gave up on the old messy code). With an all-volunteer part-time team, no budget at all, and no marketing whatsoever, we remained one of the top products in our field against competitors with massive developer staffs and multimillion-dollar revenue streams.

So how did we manage to do this? Well, for many years before I started working on the Bugzilla Project, I had been developing the seeds of a software development philosophy that wasn't just a new method of managing developers, but instead consisted of a series of universal laws—ideas that could be applied to every software project, in every language, that would resolve any situation developers might find themselves in. The problem, I figured, was that there were too many opinions in the world of software and not enough facts. If I could just figure out what the most universal and fundamental *facts* about software development were, then a lot of other problems would be laid to rest.

The Bugzilla Project was my primary test bed for figuring out these facts, and once they were determined, they made an unbelievable difference in the quality of the code and the success of the product.

It's not enough just to test out an idea on one product and call it a fact, though, no matter how successful it may be. So once I had a good idea what these facts were, I started brand-new personal projects to see the difference they would make there, and they worked just as well. Then I started to interview programmers about the situations at their organizations and the history of their software. I wanted to see if I could find counter-examples to these facts, and I found none. Instead, I learned that I could predict the end of nearly every software development story simply by hearing it halfway through, using the facts I'd discovered.

All of this is still not enough, of course. I tried out the ideas on several other real-world projects and found them equally true there as they were on Bugzilla. I presented my ideas to thousands of developers to see if anybody could come up with a counter-example from their experience, and nobody ever did. I looked up numerous experiments that had been done with software development—not to see the conclusions, which were often erroneous, but simply to see if the *data* that researchers had tracked backed up these ideas, and it completely did. I studied the history of software development and the trajectories of famous software projects to see if they matched these ideas, and they did. There is, as far as I am aware, no piece of experience or data anywhere in the history of software development that contradicts what I am about to tell you in this book.

Now, of course, I'm not saying that what is in this book is perfect. I'm just saying that it works. As far as I have been able to, I have proven that each of the ideas contained herein will improve any software project that they are applied to. Now that the ideas are formalized, I'd love to do some stronger science on them in better-crafted experiments, but until then I think they are practical enough to deliver to you as they are. I truly believe that they are the universal laws of software development, that they represent actual natural functionings of the universe in which we live, and that they have the potential to help make every software project simpler, saner, and more successful.

The strangest thing about these ideas is that they're incredibly simple. In fact, when you read some of them, you may think that they are so simple as to be stupid. It's not that people haven't known many of these ideas—it's that they didn't know they were *laws.* Once you start thinking with these ideas as *the* fundamental basis for all good software development decisions, as unshakable truths from which all best practices are derived, *that's* when you start to realize their true value.

And even if you did know these ideas—maybe every single idea in this book—think about it this way: what if all new programmers could learn all of these ideas without having to go through all the hard experiences you had to have? There are so many new programmers coming into the field right now that some companies are in a continuous confusion of bad practices resulting from inexperience. What if new developers didn't need to have all those bad experiences just to learn the fundamentals of practical software engineering? Well, I hope that is what this book represents—the opportunity for all developers, both highly experienced and brand new, to gain the most important understandings about software that there are to be had. Because here's the first fact I'm going to give you, one of the last ones I discovered:

The difference between a bad programmer and a good programmer is *understanding*.

That is, bad programmers don't understand what they are doing, and good programmers do. Believe it or not, it really is that simple. The more you understand what you are doing, the better you can do it. It applies to programming just the same as every other field in the world, except that it's more important in programming because writing software is almost purely a mental activity where understanding is everything.

Now, I'm not saying that all of the ideas in this book are going to instantly solve your problems for you, or tell you exactly what to do in your specific situation. Instead, this book will give you new ways to *think* about software development. It's up to you to use those ways of thinking to solve your own problems based on what's best for your situation. Only you can actually know enough about what's going on with your software to make correct specific decisions about it. This book just contains general principles to help guide you in making those decisions.

Even if you aren't a programmer, you may still find this book useful for several reasons:

- It is an excellent educational tool to use in software organizations.
- It will allow you to more effectively understand why software engineers want to do certain things, or why software should be developed in a certain way.
- It can help you communicate your ideas effectively to software engineers, by helping you understand the fundamental principles on which good software engineers base their decisions.

Ideally, everybody who works in the software industry should be able to read and understand this book, even if they don't have a lot of programming experience, or even if English is not their native language. Having more technical understanding will help in grasping some of the concepts, but most require no programming experience whatsoever to understand.

You'll notice, in fact, that even though this book is about software development, it contains almost no program code. How can that be? Well, the idea is that these principles should apply to any software project, in any programming language. You shouldn't have to know some specific programming language just to understand things that apply to all programming, everywhere. Instead, real-world examples and analogies are used throughout the book to help you get a better understanding of each principle, as it is presented.

Most of all, I hope that this book helps you, helps your software, and helps bring sanity, order, and simplicity into the field of software development.

Definitions, Facts, Rules, and Laws

This book contains a series of definitions, facts, rules, and laws for software development. Most of these are offset as indented, bold paragraphs in the text to highlight their importance.

- *Definitions* tell you what something is and how you would use it.
- *Facts* are just true statements about something. Any true piece of information is a fact.
- *Rules* are statements that give you true advice, cover something specific, and help guide decisions, but do not necessarily help you predict what will happen in the future or figure out other truths. They usually tell you whether or not to take some action.
- *Laws* are facts that will always be true, and that cover a broad area of knowledge. They help you figure out other important truths and allow you to predict what will happen in the future.

Out of all of these, the laws are the most important. In this book, you will know that something is a law because the text will explicitly say so. If you aren't sure what category some piece of information falls into, Appendix B lists every major piece of information in the book and labels it clearly as a law, a rule, a definition, or just a plain-old fact.

Conventions Used in This Book

The following typographical conventions are used in this book:

Italic
> Indicates new terms, URLs, email addresses, filenames, and file extensions.

`Constant width`
> Used for program listings, as well as within paragraphs to refer to program elements such as variable or function names.

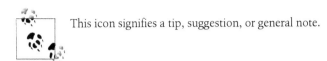 This icon signifies a tip, suggestion, or general note.

Attribution and Permissions

This book is here to help you get your job done. If you reference limited parts of it in your work or writings, we appreciate, but do not require, attribution. An attribution usually indicates the title, author, publisher, and ISBN. For example: "*Code Simplicity: The Fundamentals of Software* by Max Kanat-Alexander (O'Reilly). Copyright 2012 Max Kanat-Alexander, 978-1-4493-1389-0."

If you feel your use of examples or quotations from this book falls outside fair use or the permission given above, feel free to contact us at *permissions@oreilly.com*.

Safari® Books Online

 Safari Books Online (*http://my.safaribooksonline.com*) is an on-demand digital library that delivers expert content in both book and video form from the world's leading authors in technology and business. Technology professionals, software developers, web designers, and business and creative professionals use Safari Books Online as their primary resource for research, problem solving, learning, and certification training.

Safari Books Online offers a range of product mixes and pricing programs for organizations, government agencies, and individuals. Subscribers have access to thousands of books, training videos, and prepublication manuscripts in one fully searchable database from publishers like O'Reilly Media, Prentice Hall Professional, Addison-Wesley Professional, Microsoft Press, Sams, Que, Peachpit Press, Focal Press, Cisco Press, John Wiley & Sons, Syngress, Morgan Kaufmann, IBM Redbooks, Packt, Adobe Press, FT Press, Apress, Manning, New Riders, McGraw-Hill, Jones & Bartlett, Course Technology, and dozens more. For more information about Safari Books Online, please visit us online.

How to Contact The Author

I have a blog and website at *http://www.codesimplicity.com/* where you can see my latest thoughts about software development, make contributions, contact me for speaking engagements, submit comments and corrections, or just send me your thoughts on software development in general.

How to Contact O'Reilly

If you have general comments and questions about this book, you can send them to us at:

O'Reilly Media, Inc.
1005 Gravenstein Highway North
Sebastopol, CA 95472
800-998-9938 (in the United States or Canada)
707-829-0515 (international or local)
707-829-0104 (fax)

We have a web page for this book, where we list errata, examples, and any additional information. You can access this page at:

http://www.oreilly.com/catalog/9781449313890

To comment or ask technical questions about this book, send email to:

bookquestions@oreilly.com

For more information about our books, courses, conferences, and news, see our website at *http://www.oreilly.com*.

Find us on Facebook: *http://facebook.com/oreilly*

Follow us on Twitter: *http://twitter.com/oreillymedia*

Watch us on YouTube: *http://www.youtube.com/oreillymedia*

Acknowledgments

My editors, Andy Oram and Jolie Kanat, have been an invaluable resource. Andy's feedback was both insightful and brilliant. Jolie's insistence and support were ultimately what got this book published, and her editing work on the early drafts was appreciated.

My copyeditor, Rachel Head, has a remarkable talent for clarifying and improving everything.

Elissa Shevinsky's post-publication review changed the tone and flow of this book significantly for the better.

All the programmers that I've worked with and talked with in the open source community also deserve thanks—particularly my fellow developers on the Bugzilla Project who helped me try out all the ideas in this book on a real, live software system over the course of many years.

The comments and feedback I've received on my blog throughout the years have helped me shape the form and content of this book. Everyone who has participated there deserves thanks, even those who simply encouraged me or let me know they'd read an article.

On a personal level, I am tremendously grateful to Jevon Milan, Cathy Weaver, and everybody who works with them. In a very real sense, they are responsible for my being able to write this book. And finally, my hat's off to my friend Ron, without whom this book would not have even been possible.

Content Updates

June 13, 2012

- Re-wrote Preface and Chapter 1.
- Eliminated a chapter that used to live between Chapters 1 and 2 which wasn't necsesary to the content.
- Removed parts of what is now Chatper 2 to make it shorter.
- Fixed some formatting issues and the wording of some rules.

Introduction

All of us have been taught that software is "a series of instructions given to the computer," and this is true. However, there is no field in which a set of instructions and the result of those instructions are so closely linked as they are in the field of software development. In other fields, people write instructions and then hand them off to others, often waiting a long time to see them carried out. But when we write code, there is nobody between us and the computer. The result is *exactly* what the instructions said to do, without question. The quality of the end result is dependent entirely upon the quality of the machine, the quality of our ideas, and the quality of our code.

Of these three factors, the quality of the code is the largest problem faced by software projects today. As a result, most of this book is focuses on improving code quality. I do touch on ideas and machines as well in a few places, but mostly the focus is on improving the structure and quality of the instructions that we are giving to the machine.

However, it's important to remember that we are doing so purely because we desire a better *result*. Nothing in this book forgives a poor result—the entire reason that we focus on improving code is because *improving the code is the most important problem we must solve in order to improve the result*.

Why Simplicity?

If any appliance in my house malfunctioned as often as my computer does, I would return it. Users (and sometimes even programmers) have become used the idea that "software just has bugs." People seem to just accept that systems will bloat over time, becoming unmaintainable and unstable monstrosities that eventually have to be thrown away and re-written.

But none of this is inevitable. Instability, bloat, and various other code problems don't arise out of some natural law of the universe that requires all software to suck.

Instead, they arise almost entirely out of *complexity*.

When we start off, our software systems are small and easy to maintain. But they all grow, in time. The average software system becomes large enough that no human being could hope to hold all of its code in their mind at once. This isn't good or bad, it's just a fact. Effective software systems are, as a whole, inherently complex. The only hope we have for working with these systems is to keep the individual pieces simple, so that when we look at those pieces, we can comprehend them. Programming, in essence, must become the act of *reducing complexity to simplicity*.

If individual developers *don't* simplify the pieces of the code they work on, then those pieces become hard to understand. That makes them hard to debug, hard to modify, and hard to add features to. If too many pieces of the system become complex, the system as a whole can no longer be maintained. This is where nearly all the problems of modern software development arise from—individual developers adding complexity to the system instead of taking it away.

A good programmer should do everything in his power to make what he writes simple for other programmers to use and comprehend.

Misconceptions About Simplicity

Sometimes this idea of simplicity is misunderstood to mean that programs should not have a lot of code, or shouldn't use advanced technologies. But that's not true. Sometimes a lot of code actually leads to simplicity; it just means more writing and more reading, which is fine. And usually, advanced technologies lead to *more* simplicity, even though learning them takes time.

Some people believe that writing simple code takes more time than quickly writing something that "does the job." There is no data of which I am aware that validates this idea. Serious software development nearly always has long timelines—weeks or months at the shortest. When you add complexity into your program, you're slowing yourself down *tomorrow*. Every study that I have read (and all of my personal experience) concludes that writing simple code ultimately gets the job done faster, even when you think that complexity is a shortcut.

Software Design

A lot of this book is about software design, the process of planning out the structure of your code.

 Whenever you see the word "design" in this book, it refers to software design, not visual design, user interface design, or some other sort of design.

There's always some amount of design involved in software, even if it's just a quick decision before your fingers hit the keyboard. On a team of programmers, every person is involved in design. The lead developer is in charge of designing the overall architecture of the entire program. The senior programmers are in charge of designing their own large areas. And the junior programmers are in charge of designing their parts of the program, even if they're as simple as one part of one file. There is even a certain amount of design involved in writing a single line of code.

Everybody who writes software is a designer.

Every single person on a software team is responsible for making sure that their own code is well designed. *Nobody* who is writing code for a software project can ignore software design, at any level.

However, this does not mean that design is a democracy. You *must not* design by committee. The result will be an actively bad design—one which makes things more complex instead of simpler. Instead, all developers should have the authority to make good design decisions in their own areas. If they make poor or mediocre decisions, these should be overridden by a senior developer or the lead programmer, who should have veto power over the designers below them.[1] But otherwise, responsibility for the design of code should rest with the people who are actually working on it.

A designer should always be willing to listen to suggestions and feedback, because programmers are usually smart people who have good ideas. But after considering all the data, *any given decision must be made by an individual, not by a group of people.*

1. If you are the one overriding a decision, attempt to educate the other programmer when you do it. Show how or why your decision is better than hers. If you do this, over time you will have to override that programmer less and less. Some programmers never learn, though—if after several months or years of such education a programmer continues to make numerous bad decisions, he should be removed from your team. However, most programmers are very clever people who pick things up rapidly, so this is rarely a concern.

CHAPTER 2

The Purpose of Software

Before we can dive into the laws of software development, we have to understand what direction we're heading in with them. What's the yardstick for determining whether they work or not? Well, ideally we would have some purpose in mind. Then we could say that our ideas are valid to the degree that they accomplish that purpose.

Thus, what we need is a statement of the purpose of software itself. Not the personal purposes of the developers writing it, or the reasons the organization has for hiring programmers, but the actual purpose of *software* as a whole. Then we can see if our laws and rules help achieve that purpose.

Is it possible to derive a single statement of purpose that would fit all software? Well, I believe that I have.

The purpose of software is to help people.[1]

We can break this down to a more specific purpose for individual pieces of software. For example, a word processor exists to help people write things, and a web browser exists to help people browse the Web.

Some pieces of software exist only to help specific *groups* of people. For example, there are many pieces of accounting software that exist to help accountants; these target only that specific group of people.

What about software that helps animals or plants? Well, its purpose is really to help *people* help animals or plants.

The important thing here is that software is never there to help inanimate objects. Software does not exist to help the computer, it always exists to help people. Even when you're writing libraries, you're writing to help programmers, who are people. You are never writing to help the computer.

---

1. This fact (the purpose of all software) is more important than a law. In English, there is no simple word for this type of fact. We could perhaps call it a "senior law," even though it doesn't quite fit the criteria for a law (for example, it doesn't predict the future). For simplicity's sake, the appendixes at the end of this book list this fact as a law, and otherwise we just refer to it as "the Purpose of Software."

Now, what does "help" mean? In some ways, it's subjective—that which helps one person may not help another. But the word does have a dictionary definition, so it's not completely up to each individual what the word itself means. *Webster's New World Dictionary of the American Language* defines "help" as:

> to make it easier for (a person) to do something; aid; assist. Specifically...to do part of the work of; ease or share the labor of.

There are many things you could help with—organizing a schedule, writing a book, planning a diet, anything. *What* you help with is up to you, but the purpose is always *to help*.

The purpose of software is not "to make money" or "to show off how intelligent I am." Anybody writing with those as their only purposes is violating the purpose of software and is quite likely to get into trouble. Granted, those are ways of "helping" *yourself*, but that's a pretty limited scope of help, and designing with only those purposes in mind is likely to lead to lower-quality software than genuinely designing to help people do what they need or want to do.[2]

People who cannot conceive of helping another person will write bad software—that is, their software won't help people very much. In fact, it might be theorized (as a guess, based on observation of many programmers over time) that your *potential* ability to write good software is limited only by your ability to conceive of helping another.

Overall, when we are making decisions about software, our guiding principle can be *how we can help*. (And remember, there are varying degrees of help—one can help a lot or a little, many people or just a few.) You can even prioritize feature requests this way. Which feature will help people the most? That feature should be given the highest priority. There's more to know about prioritizing features, but "How much does it help our users?" is a good, basic question to ask about any proposed change to your software system.

In general, this purpose—to help people—is the most important thing to keep in mind when designing software, and defining it allows us now to create and understand real laws for software design.

Real-World Application

How can we apply the purpose of software to our projects in the real world? Well, let's say we're writing a text editor for programmers. The first thing we need to do is determine the purpose of our software. It's best to keep it simple, so let's say the purpose is

---

2. Note that "to make money" can certainly be one of your *personal* purposes or a purpose of your *organization*—there's nothing wrong with making money. It just shouldn't be the purpose of your *software*. In any case, the amount of money you make is likely to be directly related to how much your software helps people. In fact, the two primary factors that determine the income of a software company are probably the business skill of your organization (including administration, management, marketing, and sales) and how much your software helps people.

"to help programmers edit text." It's fine to be more specific than that, and sometimes it's helpful, but if the group can't agree on a specific purpose, at least come up with a simple one like this.

Now that we have the purpose, let's look at all of our feature requests. For each one we can ask ourselves, "How would this feature help programmers edit text?" If the answer is "It wouldn't," we can immediately cross that feature off our list. Then, for each of the remaining features, we can write down the answer as a short sentence. For example, suppose somebody asks us to add keyboard shortcuts for common actions. We could say "This helps programmers edit text because it allows them to interact with the program more quickly without taking a long break from typing." (You don't actually have to write these things down, if that doesn't seem practical for your situation —just having some idea of the answer for yourself is enough.)

There are also several other useful reasons to ask this question:

- It helps resolve uncertainties about the feature's description or how it should be implemented. For example, the answer above about keyboard shortcuts tells us that the implementation must be *fast*, because that's the value users get out of it.

- It helps the team come to an agreement about the value of a feature. Some people may not like the idea of keyboard shortcuts, but everybody should be able to agree that the answer above explains why they are valuable. In fact, some developers may even have a better idea of how to fulfill that user's need (interacting with the text editor more quickly) without keyboard shortcuts. That's fine! If the answer leads us to a better feature idea, we should implement that instead. The answer tells us what's really needed, not just what the user thought he wanted.

- Answering the question will make it obvious that some features are more important than others. This helps the project leaders prioritize work.

- At the worst, if our text editor has become bloated with too many features over time, the answer can help us decide which features should be removed.

We could also make a list of bugs, which we could look over and ask the opposite question: "How does this bug hinder programmers' editing of text?" Sometimes the answer is obvious, so it doesn't really need to be written down. For example, if the program crashes when you try to save a file, you don't need to explain why that's bad.

There are numerous other ways to apply the purpose of software in daily work; these are just a few examples.

CHAPTER 3

The Future

The primary question that faces software designers is "How do I make decisions about my software?" When faced with many possible directions you could go in, which option is the best? It's never a question of which decision would be *absolutely right* versus which decision would be *absolutely wrong*. Instead, what we want to know is, "Given many possible decisions, which of those decisions are better than others?" It's a matter of ranking decisions, and then choosing the best decision out of all the possibilities. For example, a designer might ask himself, "There are 100 different features we could work on today, but we only have the manpower to work on two. Which ones should we work on first?"

The Equation of Software Design

The above question, and indeed every question of this nature in software design, is answered by this equation:

$$D = \frac{V}{E}$$

where:

D

Stands for the *desirability* of a change. How much do we want to do something?

V

Stands for the *value* of a change. How valuable is this change? Usually, you would determine this by asking "How much does this help our users?" although there are other methods of determining value as well.

E

Stands for the *effort* involved in performing the change. How much work will the change require?

Essentially, this equation says:

The desirability of any change is directly proportional to the value of the change and inversely proportional to the effort involved in making the change.

It doesn't say whether a change is *absolutely* right or wrong; instead, it tells you how to *rank* your options. Changes that will bring a lot of value and require little effort are "better" than those that will bring little value and require a lot of effort.

Even if your question is "Should we stay the same and *not* change?" this equation tells you the answer. Ask yourself "What is the value of staying the same?" and "What is the effort involved in staying the same?" and compare that to the value of changing and the effort involved in changing.

Value

What do we mean by "value" in the equation? The simplest definition of value would be:

The degree to which this change helps anybody anywhere.

The most important people to help are your users. However, writing in features that will help you support yourself financially is also a form of value—it's valuable to you. In fact, there are many ways a change can have value; these are just two examples.

Sometimes, determining the actual, precise numerical value of any particular change is difficult. For example, say your software helps people lose weight. How do you measure the exact value of helping somebody lose weight? You can't, really. But you *can* know with precision that some features of the software will help people lose weight *a lot* and some features won't help people lose weight *at all*. So, you can still rank changes by their value.

Understanding the value of each possible change comes mostly from experience as a developer and from doing proper research with users to find out what will help them the most.

Probability of value and potential value

Value is actually composed of two factors: the *probability* of value (how likely it is that this change will help a user), and the *potential* value (how much this change will help a user during those times when it does help that person).

For example:

- A feature that could save somebody's life, even if there is only a one in a million chance of it being needed, is still a highly valuable feature. It has a high potential value (saving a life), even though it has a low probability of value.

As another example, in a spreadsheet program you might add a feature that helps blind people enter numbers into the system. Only a small percentage of people are blind, but without this feature, they couldn't use your software *at all*. Again, this feature is valuable because it has a very high potential value, despite affecting only a small group of users (a low probability of value).

- If there is a feature that will make 100% of your users smile, that is also a valuable feature. It has a very minor potential value (making people smile), but it affects a very large number of users, so it has a high probability of value.
- On the other hand, if you implement a feature that has just a one in a million chance of making somebody smile, that's not very valuable. That's a feature with low potential value and a low probability of value.

So, when considering value, you also have to consider:

- How *many* users (what percentage) will this change be valuable to?
- What is the *probability* that this feature will be valuable to a user? Or, stated another way: how *often* will this feature be valuable?
- When it is valuable, *how* valuable will it be?

Balance of harm

Some changes may cause some harm in addition to the help they bring. For example, some users may be annoyed if your software shows them ads, even if those ads help support you as a developer.

Calculating a change's value includes considering how much harm it may do, and balancing that against the help it brings.

The value of having users

Features that have no users have no immediate value. These could include features that users can't find, features that are too difficult to use, or features that simply don't help anybody. They may have value in the future, but they have no value now.

This also means that in most cases, you must actually release your software in order for it to be valuable. A change that takes too long to make can actually end up having zero value, because it doesn't get released in time to help people effectively. It can be important to take release schedules into account when determining the desirability of changes.

Effort

Effort is a little easier to put into numbers than value is. Usually, you can describe effort as "a certain number of hours of work by a certain number of people." "One hundred person-years" is an example of a commonly heard numerical measurement for effort, representing 100 years of work by 1 person, 1 year of work by 100 people, 2 years of work by 50 people, etc.

However, even though effort *can* be put into numbers, measuring it in practical situations is very tricky—perhaps impossible. Changes can have many hidden costs that can be hard to predict, such as the time you will spend in the future fixing any bugs the changes introduce. But if you are an experienced software developer, you can still rank changes by how much effort they will *probably* require, even if you don't know the exact numbers for each.

When considering the effort involved in a change, it's important to take into account *all* the effort that might be involved, not just the time you're going to spend programming. How much research will it take? How much communication will all of the developers have to do with each other? How much time will you spend thinking about the change?

In short, *every single piece* of time connected with a change is part of the effort cost.

Maintenance

The equation as we have it so far is very simple, but it is missing an important element —*time*. Not only do you have to implement a change, but you also have to maintain it over time. All changes require maintenance. This is very obvious with some changes— if you're writing a program to do people's taxes, you're going to have to update it for the new tax laws every year. But even changes that don't immediately seem to have a long-term maintenance cost *will* have one, even if it's just the cost of having to make sure that that code still works when you're testing it next year.

We must also consider value both now and in the future. When we implement some change to our system, it will help our current users, but it may also help all our future users. It may even affect the total number of future users, thus changing how much our software as a whole helps people.

Some features even change in value over time. For example, having a tax program understand the year 2009 tax laws is valuable in 2009 and 2010, but not so valuable once 2011 comes around. That's a feature that becomes less valuable over time. Some features also become more valuable over time.

So, looking at this realistically, we see that effort actually involves both the effort of *implementation* and the effort of *maintenance*, and value involves both the value *now* and the value *in the future*. In equation form, this looks like:

$$E = E_i + E_m$$

$$V = V_n + V_f$$

where:

E_i

    Stands for the *effort of implementation*.

E_m

    Stands for the *effort of maintenance*.

V_n

    Stands for *value now*.

V_f

    Stands for *future value*.

The Full Equation

With everything plugged in, the full equation looks like this:

$$D = \frac{V_n + V_f}{E_i + E_m}$$

Or, in English:

> **The desirability of a change is directly proportional to the value now plus the future value, and inversely proportional to the effort of implementation plus the effort of maintenance.**

This is the primary law of software design. However, there is a bit more to know about it.

Reducing the Equation

"Future value" and "effort of maintenance" both depend on *time*, which causes interesting things to happen with the equation when we apply it to a real-world situation. To demonstrate these, let's pretend we can use money to solve the equation for both value and effort. "Value" will be measured by how much money the change will make us. "Effort" will be measured in terms of how much money it will cost us to implement the change. You should not use the equation this way in the real world, but for the sake of our example, it's going to simplify things.

So, let's say we have a change we want to make where the equation looks like this:

$$D = \frac{\$10{,}000 + \$1000/\text{day}}{\$1{,}000 + \$100/\text{day}}$$

In other words, this change costs \$1,000 to implement (effort of implementation, bottom left) and gets us \$10,000 immediately (value now, top left). Then, each day after that, it makes us \$1,000 (future value, top right) and it costs \$100 to maintain (effort of maintenance, bottom right).

After 10 days, the accumulated future value totals $10,000, and the effort of maintenance totals $1,000. That's equal to the original "value now" and cost of implementation, after just 10 days.

After 100 days, the future value totals $100,000, and the maintenance effort comes to $10,000.

After 1,000 days, the total future value reaches $1,000,000 and the effort of maintenance totals $100,000. At this point, the original "value now" and cost of implementation look pretty tiny in comparison. As time goes on, they will become even less significant, eventually disappearing from importance entirely. Thus, as time goes on our equation reduces to this:[1]

$$D = \frac{V_f}{E_m}$$

And in fact, nearly all decisions in software design reduce entirely to measuring the future value of a change versus its effort of maintenance. There are situations in which the present value and the implementation effort are large enough to be significant in a decision, but they are extremely rare. In general, software systems are maintained for so long that the value now and the effort of implementation are guaranteed to become insignificant in almost all cases when compared to the long-term future value and effort of maintenance.

What You Do and Do Not Want

The primary lesson to learn here is that we want to avoid situations where, for a given change, the effort of maintenance will eventually outweigh the future value. For example, imagine that you implement a change where the effort and value look like this across five days:

Day	Effort	Value
1	$10	$1,000
2	$100	$100
3	$1,000	$10
4	$10,000	$1
5	$100,000	$0.10
Total	$111,110	$1111.10

1. *Optional note for mathematicians*: If you have studied calculus, you may have realized that we're starting to analyze the limit of the equation as time approaches infinity. In general, you should be thinking of the Equation of Software Design as though it were an infinite series with a limit, not just a static equation. However, for simplicity's sake, it is written here as a static equation.

Clearly, that is a terrible, terrible change that you never should have made. If things keep going at that rate, you won't be able to maintain the system at all—it will become infinitely expensive and the value you're gaining each day will become $0.

Any situation in which the effort of maintenance increases faster than the value is going to get you into trouble, even if it looks okay at first:

Day	Effort	Value
1	$1000	$1000
2	$2000	$2000
3	$4000	$3000
4	$8000	$4000
Total	**$15,000**	**$10,000**

The ideal solution—and the only way to guarantee success—is to design your systems such that the effort of maintenance *decreases* over time, and eventually becomes zero (or as close to it as possible). As long as you can do that, it doesn't matter how large or small the future value becomes; you don't have to worry about it. For example, these tables show desirable situations:

Day	Effort	Value
1	$1,000	$0
2	$100	$10
3	$10	$100
4	$0	$1,000
5	$0	$10,000
Total	**$1,110**	**$11,110**

Day	Effort	Value
1	$20	$10
2	$10	$10
3	$5	$10
4	$1	$10
5	$0	$10
Total	**$36**	**$50**

Changes with a higher future value are still *more* desirable, but as long as every decision has a maintenance cost that approaches zero over time, you can't get yourself into a dangerous future situation.

Theoretically, as long as the future value is always larger than the maintenance effort, the change is still desirable. So, you could make some change where the maintenance effort and the future value *both* increased, as long as the future value kept on being large enough to outweigh the effort of maintenance:

Day	Effort	Value
1	$1	$0
2	$2	$2
3	$3	$4
4	$4	$6
5	$5	$8
Total	$15	$20

Such a change isn't bad, but it is more desirable to make a change whose maintenance effort decreases, even if it has a larger effort of implementation. If the effort of maintenance decreases, the change actually becomes more and more desirable over time. That makes it a better choice than other possibilities.

Often, designing a system that will have decreasing maintenance effort requires a significantly larger effort of implementation—quite a bit more design work and planning are required. However, remember that the effort of implementation is nearly always an insignificant factor in making design decisions, and should mostly be ignored.

In short:

> **It is more important to reduce the effort of maintenance than it is to reduce the effort of implementation.**

That is one of the most important things there is to know about software design.

But what causes maintenance effort? How do we design systems whose maintenance effort decreases over time? That is the subject of the majority of the rest of this book. But before we get to that, we have to examine the future a little bit more.

The Quality of Design

It is very easy to write software that helps one person, right now. It is much more difficult to write software that helps millions of people now and continues to do so decades into the future. But where is most of the programming effort going to be, and when will most of those users be using the software? Right now, or in those decades to come?

The answer is that there will be far more programming work to be done—and far more users to help—in the future than in the present. Your software will have to compete and exist in the future, and the effort of maintenance and number of users will grow.

When we ignore the fact that there is a future and make things that "just work" in the present, our software becomes hard to maintain in the future. When software is hard to maintain, it's hard to make it *continue* to help people (one of our goals in software design). If you can't add new features and you can't fix problems, you eventually end up with "bad software." It stops helping its users, and it's full of bugs.

This leads us to the following rule:

> **The quality level of your design should be proportional to the length of future time in which your system will continue to help people.**

If you are writing software that will be used for only the next few hours, you don't have to put too much effort into its design. But if your software might be used for the next 10 years (and this happens far more often than you might expect, even if you think it's only going to be used for the next 6 months), then you have to put a lot of work into the design. When in doubt, design your software like it's going to be used for a long, long time: don't lock yourself into any one method of doing things, keep it flexible, don't make any decisions you can't ever change, and put a lot of attention on design.

Unforeseeable Consequences

So, when we design software, the future should be our primary focus. However, one of the most important things to know about any kind of engineering is this:

> **There are some things about the future that you do not know.**

In fact, when it comes to software design, you just can't know *most* things about the future.

> **The most common and disastrous error that programmers make is predicting something about the future when in fact they cannot know.**

For example, imagine that a programmer wrote a piece of software in 1985 that fixed broken floppy disks. It couldn't fix anything else—every single piece of it was totally dependent upon exactly how floppy disks worked. That software would now be obsolete, because people no longer use floppy disks. That programmer predicted "people will always use floppy disks"—something he *could not actually know*.

It may be possible to predict the short-term future, but the long-term future is largely unknown. The long term is also more important to us than the short term, because our design decisions will have more consequences in that longer period.

 You are safest if you don't attempt to predict the future at all, and instead make all your design decisions based on immediately known present-time information.

Now, that may sound like the exact opposite of what we've been saying so far in this chapter, but it is not. The future *is* the most important thing to consider in making design decisions. But there is a difference between designing in a way that allows for future change and attempting to *predict* the future.

As an analogy, let's say that you have a simple choice between eating and starving to death. You don't have to predict the future in order to make that choice—you know that eating is the better decision. Why? Because it will keep you alive right now, and being alive makes for a better future than being dead. The future is important, and we want to consider it in our decisions. We choose to eat now because it makes for a better future. But the future doesn't have to be *predicted*—we don't have to say something specific like "I am eating now because tomorrow I will have to save a baby's life." No matter what happens tomorrow, it will be a *better* tomorrow if you eat now rather than starve to death.

Similarly, in software design we can make certain decisions based on information that we have now, for the purpose of making a better future (decreasing maintenance effort and increasing value), without having to predict the specifics of what's going to happen in that future.

There are limited exceptions—sometimes you know exactly what is going to happen in the short-term future, and you *can* make decisions based on that. But if you're going to do that, you must be very certain about that future, and it must be very near at hand. No matter how intelligent you are, there is simply no possible way to accurately predict long-term futures.

Let's take an example outside of the realm of programming: CDs, which were designed in 1979 to replace cassette tapes as the primary method of listening to music. Who could have predicted that 20 years later, DVDs would be made in the same size and shape so that manufacturers could make CD/DVD drives for computers? And who could have imagined the problems of spinning a CD 50 times faster than it was supposed to be spun, when it was read in a CD-ROM drive?

This is why, in any type of engineering—including the field of software development —we have "guiding principles." These are certain rules that, when we follow them, keep things working well no matter what happens in the future. That is what the laws and rules of software design are—our "guiding principles" as designers.

So yes, it's important to remember that there will be a future. But that doesn't mean you have to *predict* that future. Instead, it explains *why* you should be making decisions according to the laws and rules in this book—because they lead to good future software, no matter what that future brings.

It is not even possible to predict all the ways that a particular law or rule may help you in the future—but it *will* help, and you'll be glad you applied it in your work.

You're welcome to disagree with the laws, rules, and facts you read here. Please do come to your own conclusions about them. But you should be warned that if you don't follow them, you're probably going to end up in a mess of trouble somewhere down the line, in a future you can't predict.

CHAPTER 4

Change

Now that we understand the importance of the future, and that there are some things we don't and can't know about it, what *can* we know about it?

Well, one thing you can be sure of is that as time goes on, the environment around your software is going to change. Nothing stays the same forever. This means that your software will have to change in order to adapt to the environment around it.

This gives us the Law of Change:

> **The longer your program exists, the more probable it is that any piece of it will have to change.**

As you go into an infinite future, you start tending toward a 100% probability that every single piece of your program will have to change. In the next five minutes, probably no part of your program will have to change. In the next 10 days, a small piece of it might. In the next 20 years, probably a majority of it (if not all of it) will have to change.

It's hard to predict exactly what will change, and why. Maybe you wrote a program for 4-wheeled cars, but in the future everybody will drive 18-wheel trucks. Maybe you wrote a program for high school students, but high school education will get so bad that the students can't understand it anymore.

The point is, you don't have to try to predict *what* will change; you just need to know that things *will* change. Write your software so that it's as flexible as reasonably possible, and you'll be able to adapt to whatever future changes do come along.

Change in a Real-World Program

Let's look at some data on how a real-world program changed over time. There are hundreds of files in this particular program, but the details for each file won't fit on this page, so four files have been chosen as examples. Details on these files are given in Table 4-1.

Table 4-1. Changes in files over time

	File 1	File 2	File 3	File 4
Period analyzed	5 years, 2 months	8 years, 3 months	13 years, 3 months	13 years, 4 months
Lines originally	423	192	227	309
Unchanged lines	271	101	4	8
Lines now	664	948	388	414
Grew by	241	756	161	105
Times changed	47	99	194	459
Lines added	396	1,026	913	3,828
Lines deleted	155	270	752	3,723
Lines modified	124	413	1,382	3,556
Total changes	675	1,709	3,047	11,107
Change ratio	1.6x	8.9x	13x	36x

In this table:

Period analyzed
> The time period over which the file existed.

Lines originally
> How many lines were in the file when it was originally written.

Unchanged lines
> How many lines are the same now as they were when the file was originally written.

Lines now
> How many lines there are in the file now, at the end of the analysis period.

Grew by
> The difference between "Lines now" and "Lines originally."

Times changed
> The total number of times a programmer made some set of changes to the file (where one set of changes involves changes to many lines). Usually one set of changes will represent one bug fix, one new feature, etc.

Lines added
> How many times, over the history of the file, a new line was added.

Lines deleted
> How many times, over the history of the file, an existing line was deleted.

Lines modified
> How many times, over the history of the file, an existing line was changed (but not newly added or deleted).

Total changes

The sum of the "Lines added," "Lines deleted," and "Lines modified" counts for that file.

Change ratio

How much larger "Total changes" is than "Lines originally."

When we refer to "lines" in the above descriptions, that includes every line in the files: code, comments, documentation, and empty lines. If you were to do the analysis without counting comments, documentation, and empty lines, one major difference you would see is that the "Unchanged lines" count would become much smaller in proportion to the other numbers. (In other words, the unchanged lines are nearly always comments, documentation, or empty lines.)

The most important thing to realize from this table is that a lot of change happens in a software project. It becomes more and more likely that any particular line of code will change as time goes on, but you can't predict exactly what is going to change, when it's going to change, or how much it will have to change. Each of these four files changed in very different ways (you can see this even just looking at the numbers), but they all changed a significant amount.

There are a few other interesting things about the numbers, as well:

- Looking at the change ratio, we see that more work was put into changing each file than writing it originally. Obviously, line counts aren't a perfect estimate of how much work was actually done, but they do give us a general idea. Sometimes the ratio is huge—for example, file 4 had 36 times as many total changes as it did original lines.

- The number of unchanged lines in each file is small compared to its "Lines originally" count, and even smaller compared to its "Lines now" count.

- A lot of change can happen to a file even if it only gets a little bit bigger over time. For example, file 3 grew by only 161 lines over 13 years, but during that time the total changes count reached 3,047 lines.

- The total changes count is always larger than the lines now count. In other words, you're more likely to have *changed* a line in a file than to *have* a line in a file, once the file has been around for long enough.

- In file 3, the number of lines modified is larger than the number of lines in the original file plus the number of lines added. That file's lines have been modified more often than new lines have been added. In other words, some lines of that file have changed over and over. This is common on projects with a long lifetime.

The above points aren't all that could be learned here—there is a lot more interesting analysis that could be done on these numbers. You're encouraged to dig into this data (or work out similar numbers for your own project) and see what else you can learn.

Another good learning experience is looking over the history of changes made to one particular file. If you have a record of every change made to files in your program, and you have one file that's been around for a long time, try looking at each change made over its lifetime. Think about if you could have predicted that change when the file was originally written, and consider whether the file could have been better written originally to make the changes simpler. Generally, try to understand each change and see if you can learn anything new about software development from doing so.

The Three Flaws

There are three broad mistakes that software designers make when attempting to cope with the Law of Change, listed here in order of how common they are:

1. Writing code that isn't needed
2. Not making the code easy to change
3. Being too generic

Writing Code That Isn't Needed

There is a popular rule in software design today called "You Ain't Gonna Need It," or YAGNI for short. Essentially, this rule states that you shouldn't write code before you actually need it. It's a good rule, but it's misnamed. You actually *might* need the code in the future, but since you can't predict the future you don't know how the code needs to work yet. If you write it now, before you need it, you're going to have to redesign it for your real needs once you actually start using it. So save yourself that redesign time, and simply wait until you need the code before you write it.

Another risk of writing code before you need it is that unused code tends to develop "bit rot." Since the code never runs, it might slowly become out of sync with the rest of your system and thus develop bugs, and you'll never know. Then, when you start to use it, you'll have to spend time debugging it. Or, even worse, you might trust the never-before-used code and not check it, and it may cause bugs for users. In fact, the rule here should actually be expanded to read:

> **Don't write code until you actually need it, and remove any code that isn't being used.**

That is, you should also get rid of any code that is no longer needed. You can always add it back later if it becomes needed again.

There are lots of reasons people think that they should write code before it's needed, or keep around code that isn't being used. First off, some people believe they can get around the Law of Change by programming every feature that any user could ever possibly need, right now. Then, they think, the program won't have to be changed or improved in the future. But this is wrong. It's not possible to write a system that will never change, as long as that system continues to have users.

Others believe that they are saving themselves time in the future by doing some extra work now. In some cases that philosophy works, but not when you're writing code that isn't needed. Even if that code ends up being needed in the future, you will almost certainly have to spend time redesigning it, so you're actually *wasting* time.

Writing Unnecessary Code: A Real-World Example

Once upon a time, a developer—let's call him Max (ahem)—mistakenly thought he could ignore this rule. In his program, there were drop-down boxes where users could pick a value. Every company that used the program could customize the list of choices displayed in each drop-down box. Some companies might want the choices to be names of colors. Others might want them to be names of cities. They could be anything. So, the list of valid choices needed to be stored somewhere that each company could modify it.

The obvious thing to do was just to store the list of values, and nothing else. After all, that's all that was needed. But Max decided to store two things: the list of values, and also information about whether each value was currently "active"—that is, if users could currently select that value, or if it was temporarily disabled.

However, Max never wrote any code to actually *use* the information about whether or not each field was active. All choices were active, all the time, no matter what the stored data said. He was sure that he was *just about* to write code to use the "active" information, though—maybe even tomorrow.

Several years passed, and the code to handle the "active" data didn't get written. Instead, the data just sat there, unused, confusing people and causing bugs. Numerous customers and developers wrote to Max, wondering why nothing happened when they manually edited the list of values and set choices as being inactive. One developer improperly assumed that the "active" field was in use and wrote a piece of code that used it, even though the rest of the system didn't use it. This got through to customers, and they started reporting strange bugs that took a lot of work to track down.

Eventually, some developer came along and said, "Today I will implement the ability to disable choices!" However, he discovered that the "active" field wasn't designed perfectly for his needs, so he had to do a fair bit of redesign work to implement his feature.

Net result: several bugs, lots of confusion, and extra work for the developer who *did* eventually actually need the code. And this was a relatively minor violation of the rule! Severe violations can have considerably worse consequences, including missed deadlines, major catastrophes, and possibly even the destruction of your software project.

Not Making the Code Easy to Change

One of the great killers of software projects is what we call "rigid design." This when a programmer designs code in a way that is difficult to change. There are two ways to get a rigid design:

1. Make too many assumptions about the future.
2. Write code without enough design.

Example: Making Too Many Assumptions About the Future

A government agency—let's call it The Veteran's Hospital—wants to make a program. We'll call this program "The Healthcare System." Before making this system, it decides to write a document stating exactly how the entire system should be implemented. It spends a year writing this document, making every single decision about the entire system during this time.

The developers then spend three years writing the system according to this document. As they work, they discover that the design in the document is contradictory, incomplete, and hard to implement. But the Hospital took an entire year to write it—the developers can't wait another year to have it revised. So they implement the system, following the document as closely as they can.

The system is completed and given to the users for the first time. However, the situation at the Hospital has changed dramatically in the last four years, and when the users start actually using The Healthcare System, they realize they want something completely different. But the system is made up of hundreds of thousands of lines of code, all designed rigidly according to the document—it simply can't be changed without months or years of effort.

So the Hospital starts writing a new document for a new system, and the process starts all over again.

The Hospital's mistake was attempting to predict the future. They assumed that whatever decisions they made in the document were valid for real users, and would continue to be valid when the system was completed. When the actual future arrived, it wasn't at all like what they had predicted, and their system was a multimillion dollar failure.

A better solution would have been to specify just one feature, or a tiny set of features, and immediately ask the developers to implement it. Then there could have been a back-and-forth of communication and user testing as development occurred. When the first set of features was done and released, they could have worked on additional features, one at a time, until they eventually had a system that was well designed and fully served its users' needs.

Example: Code Without Enough Design

A developer is asked to create a program that people can use to keep track of tasks they need to do. To create a new "task" in the system, users fill out a form with some information, like a short summary of the task and how far along they are on it. This stores data in a database. Then, they can make notes about their progress on the task as time goes on, and eventually note that they have completed the task.

There's a field called "Status" that indicates how far along the user is in performing the task. The values for this field are "No Work Done," "In Progress," "On Hold," and "Complete." When the Status field has the value "No Work Done," it can change only to "In Progress." When the Status field is "In Progress," it can change to "On Hold" or "Complete." And when it is "Complete," it can change only back to "In Progress."

There are 10 other fields in this program with similar rules. They each contain some different piece of information about the task (for example, to whom it's assigned, what its deadline is, and so on).

To implement these rules, the developer writes one very long, continuous piece of code with no structure, in a single file. He validates each field with custom code that is specific to that field. For example, every time he needs to check if the status is "Complete," he literally writes the word "Complete" in the code. Also, the code is not written to be reusable. Where the program has similar fields, the developer cut-and-pastes code and then modifies it slightly for the new field.

The code works. The file is 3,000 lines long. It almost entirely lacks a design.

Several months later, this developer leaves the project.

A new developer comes along and is assigned to maintain this project. He quickly discovers that this code is hard to change—if he changes one part of it, he also has to change many other parts of it in the same way in order to keep it working. To make matters even worse, the various parts are scattered around with no explanation or logical system—you have to simply read the entire file every time you want to make a change.

Customers start asking for new features. At first, the new developer does his best to implement these new features. He adds even *more* code to this file. It ends up being 5,000 lines long.

Eventually, customers start asking for features that simply can't be implemented with this design. They want to send in information about tasks by email, but this code only does it with a form. It's all designed very specifically around how the form works—it would never work with email.

Competitors start appearing that can update tasks by email. The project starts to lose its customers.

The only reason that this project survives is that two developers spend *an entire year* redesigning *just this file* so that it can be easily changed. They do their best to keep up with other feature requests while they're redesigning, but most of their time is spent on the redesign.[1]

The rule used to avoid rigid design is:

Code should be designed based on what you know now, not on what you think will happen in the future.

Design based only on your immediate, known requirements, without excluding the possibility of future requirements. If you know for a fact that you need the system to do X, and just X, then just design it to do X, right now. It might do other things that aren't X in the future, and you should keep that in mind, but for now the system should just do X.

When designing like this, it also helps to keep your individual changes small. When you only have to make a small change, it's easy to do some real design on it.

This isn't to say that planning is bad. A certain amount of planning is very valuable in software design. But even if you don't write out detailed plans, you'll be fine as long as your changes are always small and your code stays easily adaptable for the unknown future.

Being Too Generic

When faced with the fact that their code will change in the future, some developers attempt to solve the problem by designing a solution so generic that (they believe) it will accommodate every possible future situation. We call this "overengineering."

The dictionary defines overengineering as a combination of "over" (meaning "too much") and "engineer" (meaning "design and build"). So, per the dictionary, it means designing or building too much for your situation.

Wait—designing or building *too much*? What's "too much"? Isn't design a good thing?

Well, yes, most projects could use more design, as we saw in "Example: Code Without Enough Design" on page 27. But once in a while, somebody really gets into it and just goes overboard—sort of like building an orbital laser to destroy an anthill. An orbital laser is an amazing engineering feat, but it costs an enormous amount of money, takes far too long to build, and is a maintenance nightmare. Can you imagine having to go up there and fix it when it breaks?

---

1. This is the story of a file called *process_bug.cgi* from a product called "Bugzilla." The story has been simplified somewhat from what actually happened, but the numbers (in terms of lines of code and the time it took to fix it) are roughly accurate. If you want to see the entire history of the redesign project to see how it was done, you can read the records listed here: *https://bugzilla.mozilla.org/showdependencytree.cgi?id=367914&hide_resolved=0*.

There are several other problems with overengineering:

1. You can't predict the future, so no matter how generic your solution is, it will not be generic enough to satisfy the actual future requirements you will have.

2. When your code is too generic, it often doesn't handle *specifics* very well from the user's perspective. For example, say you design some code that treats all input the same—it's all just bytes. Sometimes this code processes text, and sometimes it processes pictures, but all it knows is that it's getting bytes. In a way, this is a good design: the code is simple, self-contained, small, etc.

   But then you make sure that *no* part of your code distinguishes between pictures and text. This is too generic. When the user passes in a bad picture, the error she gets is, "You passed in bad bytes." It should have said, "You passed in a bad picture," but your code is so generic that it can't tell the user that. (There are lots of ways that generic code can fall short when put to specific uses; this is just an example.)

3. Being too generic involves writing a lot of code that isn't needed, which brings us back to our first flaw.

In general, *when your design makes things more complex instead of simplifying things, you're overengineering.* That orbital laser would hugely complicate the life of a person who just needed to destroy some anthills, whereas some simple ant poison would greatly simplify that person's life by removing the ant problem (assuming it worked).

Being generic with the right things, in the right ways, can be the foundation of a successful software design. However, being *too* generic can be the cause of untold complexity, confusion, and maintenance effort. The rule for avoiding this flaw is similar to the rule for avoiding rigid designs:

Be only as generic as you know you need to be right now.

Example: Being Too Generic

In one part of a certain program, the user filled out a form and the program sent several hundred emails. This part of the program was very slow. The user would submit the form and the program would sit there for a very long time, sending all the messages.

To make this faster, the developers decided to not send all of the emails immediately. Instead, they would be sent in the background after the user submitted the form, using a pre-existing piece of code called "Email Sender."

The developer who started working on this change decided that some companies might want to use something other than Email Sender. He wrote hundreds of lines of code to allow customers to "plug in" other systems for doing background work. No customer had ever asked for this; the developer just predicted that somebody would want this specific sort of flexibility in the future.

Eventually, the Chief Architect of the program took over work on this change. He removed all of the code for "plugging in" other systems, because there was no evidence

---

that users wanted it. Thus, there was no evidence that the code should be that generic right now. With those pieces removed, the change became much simpler.

Four years have passed since the change was originally made, and not a single customer has needed the ability to plug in other systems. There was, factually, no reason to be that generic.

Incremental Development and Design

There is a method of software development that avoids the three flaws by its very nature, called "incremental development and design." It involves designing and building a system piece by piece, in order.

It is easiest to explain by example. Here's how we would use it to develop a calculator program that needs to add, subtract, multiply, and divide:

1. Plan a system that does only addition and nothing else.
2. Implement that system.
3. Fix up the now-existing system's design so that it is easy to add a subtraction feature.
4. Implement the subtraction feature in the system. Now we have a system that does only addition and subtraction, and nothing else.
5. Fix up the system's design again so that it is easy to add a multiplication feature.
6. Implement the multiplication feature in the system. Now we have a system that does addition, subtraction, multiplication, and nothing else.
7. Fix up the system's design again so that it is easy to add the division feature. (At this point, this should take little or no effort, because we already improved the design before implementing subtraction and multiplication.)
8. Implement the division feature in the system. Now we have the system we started out intending to build, with an excellent design that suits it well.

This method of development requires less time and less thought than planning the entire system up front and building it all at once. It may not be easy at first if you are used to other development methods, but it will become easy with practice.

The tricky part of using this method is deciding on the order of implementation. In general, you should pick whatever is simplest to work on at each step, when you get there. We picked addition first because it was the simplest of all four operations overall, and subtraction second because it logically built on addition in a very simple way. We could possibly have picked multiplication second, since multiplication is just the action of doing addition many times. The only thing we would *not* have picked second is division, because stepping from addition to division is too far of a logical jump—it's too complex. On the other hand, stepping from multiplication to division at the end was really very simple, so that was a good choice.

Sometimes you may even need to take a single feature and break it down into many small, simple, logical steps so that it can be implemented easily.

This is actually a combination of two methods: one called "incremental development" and another called "incremental design." Incremental development is a method of building up a whole system by doing work in small pieces. In our list, each step that started with "Implement" was part of the incremental development process. Incremental design is similarly a method of creating and improving the system's *design* in small increments. Each step that started with "Fix up the system's design" or "Plan" was part of the incremental design process.

Incremental development and design is not the *only* valid method of software development, but it is one that definitely prevents the three flaws outlined in the previous section.

Defects and Design

Unfortunately, no programmer is perfect. Good programmers will introduce roughly one defect into a program for every 100 lines of code they write. The best programmers, under the best possible circumstances, will introduce one defect per 1,000 lines of code they write.

In other words, no matter how good or bad you are as a programmer, it's certain that the more you code, the more defects you will introduce. This allows us to state a law called the Law of Defect Probability:

> **The chance of introducing a defect into your program is proportional to the size of the changes you make to it.**

This is important because defects violate our purpose of helping people, and therefore should be avoided. Also, fixing defects is a form of maintenance. Thus, increasing the number of defects increases our effort of maintenance.

With this law, without having to predict the future, we can immediately see that making small changes is likely to lead to lower maintenance effort than making large changes would. Small changes = fewer defects = less maintenance.

This law is also sometimes stated more informally as "You can't introduce new bugs if you don't add or modify code."

The funny thing about this law is that it seems to be in conflict with the Law of Change —your software has to change, but changing it will introduce defects. That is a real conflict, and it's balancing these laws that requires your intelligence as a software designer. It is actually that conflict that explains why we *need* design, and in fact tells us what the ideal design is:

> **The best design is the one that allows for the most change in the environment with the least change in the software.**

And that, pretty simply, sums up much of what is known about good software design today.

If It Ain't Broken...

Okay, so you can't introduce bugs into your program if you don't add or modify code, and that's a major law of software design. However, there's also a very important related rule that many software engineers have heard in one form or another, but sometimes forget:

Never "fix" anything unless it's a problem, and you have evidence showing that the problem really exists.

It's important to have *evidence* of problems before you address them. Otherwise, you might be developing features that don't solve anybody's problem, or you might be "fixing" things that aren't broken.

If you fix problems without evidence, you're probably going to break things. You're introducing change into your system, which is going to bring new defects along with it. And not just that, but you're wasting your time and adding complexity to your program for no reason.

So what counts as "evidence"? Suppose five users report that when they push the red button, your program crashes. Okay, that's evidence enough! Alternatively, you may push the red button yourself and notice that the program crashes.

However, just because a user reports something doesn't mean it's a problem. Sometimes the user will simply not have realized that your program had some feature already, and so asked you to implement something else unnecessarily. For example, say you write a program that sorts a list of words alphabetically, and a user asks you to add a feature that sorts a list of *letters* alphabetically. Your program already does that. Actually, it already does more than that—this is often the case, with this sort of confused request. In this case, the user may think there is a problem when there isn't. He may even present "evidence" that he can't sort a list of letters, when in fact the problem is just that he didn't realize that he should use the *word*-sorting feature.

 If you get a lot of requests like the above, it means that users can't easily find the features they need in your program. That's something you should fix.

Sometimes a user will report that there's a bug, when actually it's the program behaving exactly as you intended it to. In this case, it's a matter of majority rules. If a significant number of users think that the behavior is a bug, it's a bug. If only a tiny minority (like one or two) think it's a bug, it's not a bug.

The most famous error in this area is what we call "premature optimization." That is, some developers seem to like to make things go fast, but they spend time optimizing their code before they know that it's slow! This is like a charity sending food to rich people and saying, "We just wanted to help people!" Illogical, isn't it? They're solving a problem that doesn't exist.

The only parts of your program where you should be concerned about speed are the exact parts that you can show are causing a real performance problem for your users. For the rest of the code, the primary concerns are flexibility and simplicity, not making it go fast.

There are infinite ways of violating this rule, but the way to follow it is simple: just get real evidence that a problem is *valid* before you address it.

Don't Repeat Yourself

This is probably the most well known rule in software design. You probably already know it. But it is valid, and so it is included here:

In any particular system, any piece of information should, ideally, exist only once.

Let's say you have a field called "Password" that appears on 100 screens of your program's user interface. What if you want to change the name of the field to "Passcode"? Well, if you have stored the name of the field in one central location in your code, fixing it will require a one-line code change. But if you wrote the word "Password" manually into all 100 screens of the user interface, you'll need to make 100 changes to fix it.

This also applies to blocks of code. You should not be copying and pasting blocks of code. Instead, you should be using the various pieces of programming technology that allow one piece of code to "use," "call," or "include" another piece of existing code.

One of the good reasons to follow this rule is the Law of Defect Probability. If we can reuse old code, we don't have to write or change as much code when we add new features, so we introduce fewer defects.

It also helps us with flexibility in our designs. If we need to change how our program works, we can change some code in just one place, instead of having to go through the whole program and make multiple changes.

A lot of good design is based on this rule. That is, the more clever you can get with making code "use" other code and centralizing information, the better your design is. This is another area where your intelligence really comes to play in programming.

CHAPTER 6

Simplicity

Okay, so if we never change our software, we can entirely avoid defects. But change is inevitable, particularly if we're going to add new features. So "don't change anything" can't be the ultimate defect reduction technique.

As explained in Chapter 5, if you want to avoid defects in your code, it does help to keep your changes small. But if you want to go further and eliminate defects even from your small changes, there's another law that can help you. And it doesn't just reduce defects—it keeps your code maintainable, makes it easy to add new features, and improves the overall understandability of your code. This is the Law of Simplicity:

> **The ease of maintenance of any piece of software is proportional to the simplicity of its individual pieces.**

That is, the simpler the pieces are, the more easily you can change things in the future. *Perfect* ease of maintenance is impossible, but it's the goal you strive for—total change or infinite new code with no difficulty.

You may have noticed that this law doesn't talk about the simplicity of the *whole system*, though, only the *individual pieces*. Why?

Well, an average-sized computer program is so complex that no human being could comprehend it all at once. It's only possible to comprehend pieces of it. So we actually always have some large, complex structure for our whole program. What then becomes important is that the pieces can be understood when we look at them. The simpler the pieces are, the more likely it is that any given person will understand them. That's particularly important when you're handing your code off to other people, or when you go away from your code for a few months and then have to come back and relearn what you did.

An Architecture Analogy

Imagine that you're building a 30-foot-tall steel structure. You could make it out of a bunch of small girders, which are simple pieces. Or you could forge three huge, complex pieces of steel, and put them together.

With the girders approach, it's easy to make or buy the individual pieces. And if one breaks, you just replace it with an identical spare part. Construction is simple, and so is maintenance.

The three huge pieces, on the other hand, have to be carefully custom-made and worked on extensively. Each completed piece is so large that it's hard to find and fix all its defects. And if, after the building is finished, you discover numerous flaws in each piece, you can't replace them—the building would fall over if you took any piece out. So you have to weld on ugly patches of metal and hope that the whole thing stays up.

Software is very similar—when you write your code in simple, self-contained pieces, fixing defects and maintaining the system are easy. When you design large, complex chunks, each piece takes a lot of work and doesn't get as much polish as it should. The system becomes hard to maintain, and patches and hacks have to be added constantly to keep it running.

So why do people sometimes write software in large, complex chunks instead of in small, simple pieces? Well, there's a perceived time savings with the huge pieces method when you're first creating the software. With a bunch of small pieces, a lot of time is spent putting them together. You don't see that with the huge pieces—there are a few of them, they snap together, and that's it.

However, the quality of the huge pieces system is much lower, and you will spend a lot of time fixing it in the future. It will become harder and harder to maintain, while the simple system becomes easier and easier. In the long run, it's simplicity that's efficient, not complexity.

So how do we use this law, in the practical world of programming? That's the subject of much of the rest of this book. In general, though, the idea is to make the individual components of your code as simple as possible, and then make sure they stay that way over time.

One good way to do this is to use the incremental development and design method introduced at the end of Chapter 4. Since there is a "redesign" step before each new feature is added, you can use that time to simplify the system. Even if you're not using that method, though, you can take some time between adding features to simplify any pieces that seem too complex to you or your fellow developers.

One way or another, you often have to take what you've created and make it simpler —you can't rely on your initial design always being the right one. You have to redesign pieces of the system continuously as new situations and requirements arise.

Granted, this can be a fairly difficult task. You aren't always given simple tools to write your programs with—the languages are complex, the computer itself is complex, etc. But strive for simplicity with what you have.

Simplicity and the Equation of Software Design

You may have realized this, but this law tells us the most important thing we can do right now that will reduce the effort of maintenance in the Equation of Software Design —make our code simpler. We don't have to predict the future to do that; we can just look at our code, see if it is complex, and make it less complex for ourselves right now. *This* is how you get an effort of maintenance that decreases over time—you continually work to make your code simpler.

There is a certain amount of work involved in doing this simplification, but overall it is far easier to make changes in a simple system than in a complex system—so you spend a little time doing the simplification now to save a lot of time later.

As you decrease the effort of maintenance for your system, you increase the desirability of all possible changes. (Go back to Chapter 3 and take another look at the Equation of Software Design if you want to refresh your memory about the details.) Simplifying your code decreases the effort of maintenance, thereby increasing the desirability of every other possible change.

Simplicity Is Relative

Okay, so we want things to be simple. However, how you define "simple" really depends on your target audience. What is simple to you might not be simple to your coworkers. Also, when *you* create something, it may seem relatively "simple" to you, because you understand it inside and out. But to somebody who's never seen it before, it might appear very complicated.

If you want to understand the viewpoint of somebody who doesn't know anything about your code, find some code you've never read, and read it. Try to understand not just the individual lines, but what the whole program is doing and how you would modify it if you had to. That's the same experience other people are having when reading your code. You might notice that the level of complexity doesn't have to get very high before it becomes frustrating to read other people's code.

That's why it's good to have sections in your code documentation like "New to This Code?" that contain some simple explanations that will help people understand your code. These should be written as if the reader knows nothing about the program, because if people are new to something, they probably *don't* know anything about it.

Way too many software projects mess this up. You go to read the documentation written for developers, and you're presented with a huge mass of links and no direction. This appears simple to the long-time developer of the project, because a page with lots of links lets that developer quickly go to the part he's looking for. But for someone new to the project, it's complicated. On the other hand, for the long-time developer, adding a page with big, simple buttons and eliminating that list of links would add to the complexity of his task, because his main goal will just be to find a very specific thing very fast in the documentation.

The only thing worse than complex documentation is *no* documentation, where you're just expected to figure it out for yourself or "already know" how the code works. To the developer, the way his program works is obvious, but to others it's totally unknown.

Context is important, too. For example, in the context of program code, advanced technologies often lead to simplicity, if used right. But imagine if such a program's advanced internal structure were displayed directly on a web page as the only interface to the program—it wouldn't be simple in that context, even to the developer!

Sometimes what seems complex in one context is simple in another. Displaying a lot of explanatory text on a billboard by the side of the road would be overly complex—there's just no time for passing drivers to read all that text, so it would be stupid to put it there. But in a manual for a computer program, including lots of explanatory text would be a lot simpler than just giving a one-sentence description of something. That's why this book doesn't have just one-line chapters; it wouldn't really be all that simple to just say something and then not explain it.

With all these different viewpoints and contexts to consider, does this mean that achieving simplicity is impossibly difficult? No! Not at all. There are specific target audiences for everything, and the context of any individual thing you're doing is usually pretty limited. The problem is always solvable. It's just important to take these considerations into account when designing your software, so that when someone actually comes to use it, it really is simple for that particular person.

The Editor War

There have been numerous arguments in the world of software development about what the best tools for a job are. People love different text editors, different programming languages, different operating systems, etc. Perhaps the most famous "war" in software development is between the users of two particular text editors, *vi* and Emacs. Users of each have sometimes claimed that their preferred editor is fundamentally superior to the other.

In reality, there is rarely a fundamentally superior tool for writing software; there is only a tool that particular people find to be simpler for the task at hand. Emacs users find Emacs to be the simplest tool to use for writing software, and *vi* users find *vi* to be the simplest. To some degree, this has to do with fundamental differences between individuals in terms of how they like to work or how they think. People simply have different preferences, and there's no right or wrong. But to a larger degree, the perceived simplicity of a tool has to do with familiarity—anybody who has used a particular tool for a long time has likely become very familiar with it, which makes it much simpler than any other tool, from that person's viewpoint. In order for a new tool to seem equally simple, that tool would have to be *extremely* simple, and programmers' text editors rarely are.

Non-programmers would likely consider *both* text editors to be complex beyond reason, which is another example of how simplicity is relative.

 Tools *can* have problems that make them unsuitable for the task at hand or the wrong choice for software design reasons (see "Bad Technologies" on page 52 in Chapter 7). But barring those problems, the *relative simplicity* of a tool is what will allow an individual programmer to determine what is best for a given situation.

How Simple Do You Have to Be?

When you're working on a project, questions about simplicity can arise. How simple do we really have to be? Just how much do we have to simplify this thing? Is it simple enough?

Well, of course, simplicity is relative. But even so, you can still achieve *more* or *less* simplicity. From the relative viewpoint of your user, your product can be hard to use, easy to use, or somewhere in between. Likewise, from the viewpoint of another programmer, your code can be relatively hard or easy to read.

So, how simple do you have to be?

Honestly?

If you really want to succeed?

Stupid, dumb simple.

The nice thing about that level of simplicity is that, for the most part, anything usable by normal people is also usable by geniuses. You get a much broader range of possible users.

But often, people really just don't understand how stupid, dumb simple they have to be to get to that level. Let's look at an example. When you're at the mall, there are maps that tell you where everything is. On the best mall maps, there is a huge red dot, with the words "YOU ARE HERE" in gigantic letters, right in front of you. On the poorer maps, there is a tiny yellow triangle in the middle of the map that is very hard to find, and off to the side there's some text that explains, "The tiny yellow triangle means 'You are here!'" Add this to the general confusion of trying to find anything on these maps, and you could be spending five or six minutes just standing in front of the thing, trying to figure out how to get where you're going.

To the guy that designed the map, this may seem totally reasonable. He spent lots of time designing it, so it was clearly important enough to him that he would be happy to spend several minutes looking at it, learning all about it, figuring it out, etc. But to us, the people who are actually *using* the map, it's a very, very minor part of our existence. We just want it to be as simple as possible, so that we can use it quickly and get on with our lives!

Many programmers are particularly bad about this with their code. They assume that other programmers will be willing spend a lot of time learning all about their code, because after all, it took a lot of time to write it! The code is important to them, so won't it be important to everybody?

Now, programmers are generally an intelligent bunch. But it's still a mistake to think, "Oh, other programmers will understand everything I've done here without any simplification or explanation of my code." It's not a matter of intelligence—it's a matter of *knowledge*. Programmers who are new to your code don't know anything about it; they have to learn. The easier you make it for them to learn, the faster they are going to figure it out, and the easier it will be for them to use it.

There are lots of ways to make your code easy to learn: simple documentation, simple design, step-by-step tutorials, etc.

But, if your code isn't stupid, dumb simple to learn, people are going to have trouble with it. They're going to use it incorrectly, create bugs, and generally muck things up. And when all this happens, who are they going to come ask about it? Yes, you! *You* are going to be spending time answering all of their questions. (Mmm, sounds fun, doesn't it?)

None of us like being talked down to or treated like we're idiots. And sometimes that leads us to create things that are a little complicated, so that we feel like we aren't talking down to the user or to other programmers. We throw in some big words, make it a little less than simple, and people respect our intelligence but *feel kind of stupid because they* **don't get it**. They might think we're way smarter than they could ever be, and that is kind of flattering. But really, is that helping *them*?

On the other hand, when you make your product or code stupidly simple, you're allowing people to understand it. That makes them feel smart, lets them do what they're trying to do, and doesn't reflect badly on you at all. In fact, people will probably admire you *more* if you make things simple than if you make them complex.

Now, your whole family does not have to be able to read your code. Simplicity is still relative, and the target audience for code is *other programmers*. But to those other programmers, your code should seem very simple and easy to understand. It can use as much advanced technology as is required to achieve that simplicity, but it should still ultimately be simple.

When the question "How simple do I have to be?" comes up, you might as well ask yourself, "Do I want people to understand this and be happy, or do I want them to be confused and frustrated?" If you pick the former, there's only one level of simplicity that will assure your success: *Stupid, dumb simple*.

Be Consistent

Consistency is a big part of simplicity. If you do something one way in one place, do it that way in every place.

If you name a variable somethingLikeThis, then all of your variables should be named that way (otherVariable, anotherNameLikeThat, etc.). If you have variables that are named_like_this, then all variables should be all lowercase and have underscores between the words.

Code that isn't consistent is harder for a programmer to understand and read.

We can illustrate this by looking at an example from natural language. Compare these two sentences:

- This is a normal sentence with normal words that everybody can understand.
- tHisisanOrmalseNtencewitHnorMalwordsthAtevErybOdycAnunderStaNd.

Both of those sentences say the exact same thing, but the first one is way simpler to read because it's consistent with how most people write English. Sure, it is *possible* to read the second sentence, but would you want to read a whole book written like that? Right. So, would you want to read a whole program written without any consistency?

There are situations in programming where it doesn't matter how you do things, as long as you *always* do them that way. Theoretically, you could write your code in some crazy complex way, but as long as you were *consistent* with it, people would learn how to read it. (Of course, it's better to be consistent and simple, but if you can't be totally simple, at least be consistent.)

Total consistency can also make programming easier in many cases. For example, if every object in your program has a field called name, you can write one piece of simple code that deals with the name field of every object in your entire program. But if in Object A the name field is called a_name and in Object B it's called name_of_mine, you'll have to write special code to deal with Object A and Object B differently.

Similarly, your program should *behave* in a consistent fashion internally. A programmer who is familiar with how to use one part of your code should be immediately familiar with how to use another part of your code, because both pieces behave in a similar fashion. For example, if when using Part A the programmer has to call three functions and then write some code, when using Part B she should also have to call a similar set of three functions and then write some code. And if you have a function named dump in Part A that causes Part A to print out all its internal variables, the function named dump in Part B should do the same thing for Part B. Don't keep forcing programmers to relearn the way your system works every time they look at a new piece of it.

Maybe things aren't that consistent in the real world, but you're in charge of the world of your program, so you can make things simple and consistent.

There are some examples of consistency in the real world. In much of Asia, people use chopsticks to eat. In the Americas and Europe, people use forks. Okay, that's two different methods of eating, but overall it's pretty consistent, in any given area. Now imagine if every time you went to somebody's house, you had to learn some whole new way of eating. Maybe at Bob's house they eat with scissors, and at Mary's house they eat with flat pieces of cardboard. Eating would get pretty complex, wouldn't it?

It's the same in programming—without consistency, things get very complex. With consistency, they become simple. And even if they're not simple, at least you can learn the complexity just once, and then you know it forever.

Readability

As has been said many times in the world of software development, code is read more often than it is written. So, it's important to make code easy to read:

> **Readability of code depends primarily on how space is occupied by letters and symbols.**

If the whole universe were black, you wouldn't be able to tell objects apart. They'd all be a single black mass. Just the same, if a whole file is a mass of code without enough consistent, logical spacing, it's hard to separate out the pieces. Space is what keeps things separate.

You don't want too much space, because then it's hard to tell how things are related. And you don't want too little, because then it's hard to tell that things are separate.

There's no hard and fast rule about exactly how code should be spaced, except that it should be done in a consistent manner and the spacing should help inform the reader about the code's structure.

Example: Spaces

This code is hard to read because it has too little space in it—very little information about the code's structure is provided:

```
x=1+2;y=3+4;z=x+y;if(z>y+x){print"error";}
```

Here's the same block of code with too much space in it—the space hinders the reader from seeing the code's structure:

```
x               =       1+      2;
y = 3                +4;

    z = x   +       y;
if (z  >      y+x)
    {          print "error" ;
             }
```

That's even harder to read than the code with *no* space.

Here's the same code with reasonable spacing:

```
x = 1 + 2;
y = 3 + 4;
z = x + y;
if (z > y + x) {
    print "error";
}
```

That's much easier to read, and it helps you realize how the programmer intended the program to be designed. Three variables are set, and then in some condition, an error is thrown. That's the structure of the system, made clear to the reader by the way the programmer used space.

Making code easy to read also helps make it easy to fix. In the previous example, when the code is properly spaced, we can easily see that z will never be greater than y + x, because z is always equal to y + x. Thus, the block starting with if (z > y + x) should be deleted, as it's unnecessary.

In general, if you have some very buggy code that is also hard to read, the first thing you should do is make it more readable. Then you can see more clearly where the bugs are.

Naming Things

An important part of readability is giving good names to variables, functions, classes, etc. Ideally:

> **Names should be long enough to fully communicate what something is or does without being so long that they become hard to read.**

It's also important to think about how the function, variable, etc. is going to be used. Once we start putting its name into lines of code, will it make those lines of code so long that they're hard to read? For example, if you have a function that is only called once, on one line all by itself (with no other code in that line), it can have a fairly long name. However, a function that you're going to use frequently in complex expressions should probably have a name that is short (though still long enough to fully communicate what it does).

Comments

Having good comments in code is a big part of making it readable. However, you generally should not add comments that say *what* a piece of code is doing. That should be obvious from reading the code. If it *isn't* obvious, the code should be made simpler. Only if you can't make code simpler should you have a comment explaining what it does.

The real purpose of comments is to explain *why* you did something, when the reason isn't obvious. If you don't explain that, other programmers may be confused, and when they go to change your code they might remove important parts of it if those parts don't seem to have a reason to exist.

Some people believe that readability is the be-all and end-all of code simplicity—that if your code is easy to read, you've done all you need to do as a designer. That's not true—you can have very readable code and still have a system that is too complex. However, making your code readable *is* very important, and it's usually the first step that should be taken on the road to good software design.

Simplicity Requires Design

Unfortunately, people do not naturally build simple systems. Without attention paid to design, a system will evolve into a massive, complicated beast.

If your project lacks a good design, and it continues to grow, you will eventually end up over your head in complexity. This is hard for certain people to imagine—some can't imagine that there is a future beyond lunch, and others just haven't had enough experience to understand how complex things can get. And there can be a corporate culture that says, "Oh, we just hack in new features; we should do things the right way, but we can't because *blah blah blah*." But one day, your project will fail. And no matter how many *reasons* you can give for that failure, it won't change the fact that your project *failed.*

On the other side of things, when you've designed well, there's often not a whole lot of credit that comes your way. Catastrophic failures in design are big and noticeable, whereas small increments of work toward a good design are invisible to people who aren't intimately connected with the code. This can make being a designer a difficult job. Handling a big failure gets you a lot of thanks, but preventing one from ever happening...well, nobody's likely to notice.

So, let's congratulate you here. Did you think a bit about design? Great! Your users and fellow developers will see the benefits—working software, on-time releases, and a clear, understandable codebase. You will feel confident in your own work and go home feeling accomplished. Will the other developers know how much work it took to make things run so smoothly? Maybe not. But that's okay. There are other rewards in the world besides the congratulations of your peers.

Once in a rare while, though, you will get some appreciation for all of your work. Don't despair—somebody *will* notice eventually. And until then, enjoy all of the other positive results of effective, correct design.

 When you start applying the design principles in this book to your project, it may take some of your junior programmers or colleagues a long time to understand why they should also design well. Having them read this book will help. If they can't or won't read it, keep guiding them (or forcing them, at the worst) toward good design decisions, and they will see after a couple of years (at the outside) how well good design decisions pay off.

CHAPTER 7

Complexity

When you work as a professional programmer, chances are you'll know somebody (or you are somebody!) who's going through this common development horror story: "We started working on this project five years ago, and the technology we were using/making was modern then, but it's obsolete now. Things keep getting more and more complex with this obsolete technology, so it keeps getting less and less likely that we'll ever finish the project. But if we rewrite, we could be here for another five years!"

Another popular one is: "We can't develop fast enough to keep up with modern user needs." Or, "While we were developing, Company X wrote a product better than ours much more quickly than we did."

We know now that the source of these problems is *complexity*. You start out with a simple project that can be completed in one month. Then you add complexity, and the task will take three months. Then you take each piece of that and make it more complex, and the task will take *nine* months.

Complexity builds on complexity—it's not just a linear thing. That is, you can't make assumptions like: "We have 10 features, so adding 1 more will only add 10 percent more time." In fact, that one new feature will have to be coordinated with all 10 of your existing features. So, if it takes 10 hours of coding time to implement the feature itself, it may well take another 10 hours of coding time to make the 10 existing features all interact properly with the new feature. The more features there are, the higher the cost of adding a feature gets. You can minimize this problem by having an excellent software design, but there will still always be some slight extra cost for every new feature.

Some projects start out with such a complex set of requirements that they never get a first version out. If you're in this situation, you should just trim features. Don't shoot for the moon in your first release—get out something that works and make it work better over time.

There are other ways to add complexity than just adding features, too. The most common other ways are:

Expanding the purpose of the software

Generally, just don't ever do this. Your marketing department might be drooling over the idea of making a single piece of software that does your taxes and cooks dinner, but you should be screaming as loud as you can whenever any suggestion like that comes near your desk. Stick to the existing purpose of your software—it just has to do what it does *well*, and you will succeed (as long as your software helps people with something they actually need and want help with).

Adding programmers

Yes, that's right—adding more people to the team does not make things simpler; instead, it adds complexity. There's a famous book called *The Mythical Man Month* by Fred Brooks, that points this out. If you have 10 programmers, adding an eleventh means spending time to groove in that one programmer, plus time to groove in the existing 10 programmers to the new person, plus the time spent by the new person interacting with the existing 10 programmers, and so on and so on. You are more likely to be successful with a small group of expert programmers than a large group of inexpert programmers.

Changing things that don't need to be changed

Any time you change something, you're adding complexity. Whether it's a requirement, a design, or just a piece of code, you're introducing the possibility of bugs, as well as the time required to decide upon the change, the time required to implement the change, the time required to validate that the new change works with all the other pieces of the software, the time required to track the change, and the time required to test the change. Each change builds on the last in terms of all this complexity, so the more you change, the more time each new change is going to take. It's still important to make certain changes, but you should be making informed decisions about them, not just making changes on a whim.

Being locked into bad technologies

Basically, this is where you decide to use some technology, and then are stuck with it for a long time because you're so dependent on it. A technology in this sense is "bad" if it locks you in (doesn't allow you to switch easily to some other technology in the future), isn't going to be flexible enough for your future needs, or just doesn't have the level of quality you need in order to design simple software with it.

Misunderstanding

Programmers who don't fully understand their work tend to develop complex systems. It can become a vicious cycle: misunderstanding leads to complexity, which leads to further misunderstanding, and so on. One of the best ways to improve your design skills is to be sure that you fully understand the systems and tools you are working with. The better you understand these, and the more you know about software in general, the simpler your designs can be.

Poor design or no design

Basically, this just means "a failure to plan for change." Things are going to change, and design work is required to maintain simplicity while the project grows. You have to design well at the start and keep on designing well as the system expands —otherwise, you can introduce massive complexity very fast, because with a poor design, each new feature *multiplies* the complexity of the code instead of just *adding* a little bit to it.

Reinventing the wheel

If, for example, you invent your own protocol when a perfectly good one exists, you're going to be spending a lot of time working on the protocol, when you could just be working on your software. You should almost never have any huge invented-in-house dependency, like a web server, a protocol, or a major library, unless that *is* your product. The only times it's okay to reinvent the wheel are when any of the following are true:

a. You need something that doesn't exist yet.

b. All of the existing "wheels" are bad technologies that will lock you in.

c. The existing "wheels" are fundamentally incapable of handling your needs.

d. The existing "wheels" aren't being properly maintained and you can't take over maintenance of them (because, for example, you don't have the source code).

All of these factors are *slowly and gradually* harmful to your project, not immediately destructive. Most of them only do long-term damage—something you won't see for a year or more—so when somebody proposes them, often they sound harmless. And even when you start implementing them, they may seem fine. But as time goes on— and particularly as more and more of these stack up—the complexity becomes more apparent and grows and grows and grows, until you're another victim of that ever-so-common horror story, *The Never-Shipping Product*.

Complexity and Purpose

The basic purpose of any given system that you're working on should be pretty simple. That helps keep the system as a whole as simple as it can realistically be. But if you start to add features that fulfill some *other* purpose, things get very complex very quickly. For example, the basic purpose of a word processor is to help you write things. If we suddenly made it also able to read your email, it would get ridiculously complicated. Can you imagine what the user interface would look like? Where would you put all the buttons? We would say that this is a *violation* of your word processor's purpose. You didn't even expand its purpose; you just added features that have nothing to do with it.

It's also important to think about the *user's* purpose. Your user will be trying to do something. Ideally, the purpose of a program should be very close (in the exact words you'd use to describe it) to the user's purpose. For example, let's say the user's purpose is to do her taxes. She wants software whose purpose is to help people do their taxes.

If your purpose and the user's purpose don't match up, you're probably making her life difficult. For example, if she wants to read her email, but the primary purpose of the program she's using is to show ads to users, those purposes are not matched up.

Want to see your user get angry really fast? Make it difficult for her to accomplish her purpose. Pop up windows in her face when she's trying to do something. Add so many features to your program that she can't find the right one. Use lots of strange icons that she doesn't understand. There are lots of ways to do it, but they all boil down to interfering with the user's purpose or violating the basic purpose of the program itself.

Sometimes, marketers or managers have goals for a program that are not really aligned with the basic purpose of the program, like "be cute," "have an edgy design," "become popular with the news media," "use the latest technologies," and so on. These people may be important to your organization, but they are not the people who should be deciding what your program does! As a software designer or technical manager, it's *your* job to see that the program stays on track and never violates its basic purpose. Nobody else is going to hold that responsibility. Sometimes you might really have to fight for it, but it's well worth it in the long run.

And it's not as if you'd come to a marketing failure with that philosophy. There are many, many products that have been extremely successful by sticking to just one purpose. Soap's purpose is just to clean things. Salt just makes things salty. A light bulb just lights things up. But all of these are products that have supported enormous corporations for decades. You don't have to have a complicated product to have effective marketing—you just have to have knowledge and skill in marketing, which is a completely separate field from software design.

Really, there's no need to get fancy and complex and try to do 500 things at once in a single program. Users are happiest with a focused, simple product that never violates its basic purpose.

Bad Technologies

Another common source of complexity is picking the wrong technology to use in your system—particularly one that ends up not holding up well to future requirements. However, it can be tricky to know, without being able to predict the future, what technology you *should* choose now. Thankfully, there are three factors you can look at to determine if a technology is "bad" before you even start using it: *survival potential*, *interoperability*, and *attention to quality*.

Survival Potential

A technology's survival potential is the likelihood that it will continue to be maintained. If you get stuck with a library or some dependency that becomes obsolete and unmaintained, you're really in for some trouble.

You can get some idea of the survival potential of a piece of software by looking at its recent release history. Have the developers been frequently coming out with new versions that solve real user problems? Also, how responsive are the developers to bug reports? Do they have a mailing list or a support team that's very active? Are there lots of people online talking about this technology? If a technology has a lot of momentum now, you can be fairly sure that it's not going to die any time soon.

Also look at whether just one vendor is pushing the technology, or if it's broadly accepted and used across many areas of software by many different developers. If there is only one vendor who pushes and forwards the system, there's a risk that that vendor will either go out of business or just decide to stop maintaining the system.

Popularity

It may sound like we're saying you should just pick the most popular technology that suits your needs. To some degree, this is true—popular technologies have a lot of survival potential. However, you have to look at the difference between tools that are *validly* popular, and tools that are popular only because they hold some sort of monopoly.

At the time of this book's writing, C is one example of a validly popular language. Many people use it at many different organizations for many different purposes. It's the subject of several international standards, and there are numerous implementations of those standards, including many different widely used compilers.

Some technologies are popular only because you *must* use them, though.[1] Suppose Company X designs its own programming language. Then it designs a popular device that accepts only programs written in that language. This is the "one vendor" case mentioned in the text—the language may seem popular, but it actually has poor survival potential unless it gets picked up broadly across the software industry.

Interoperability

Interoperability is a measure of how easy it is to switch away from a technology if you have to. To get an idea of the interoperability of a technology, ask yourself, "Can we interact with this technology in some standard way, so it would be easy to switch to another system that follows the same standard?"

---

1. Developers can be very passionate about technologies they work with. To avoid offending users of certain technologies, no specific technology is mentioned here.

For example, there are international standards for how a program should interact with a database system. Some database systems support these standards very well. If you pick one of these good database systems, you can switch to another database system in the future with only minor changes to your program.

However, some other database systems aren't very good at supporting standards. If you want to switch between database systems that don't support standards, you'll have to rewrite your program. So, when you choose one of these nonstandard systems, you are locked into it and will be unable to easily switch to a different system.

Attention to Quality

This one is more of a subjective measurement, but the idea is to see if the product has been getting better in its recent releases. If you can see the source code, check if the developers are refactoring and cleaning up the codebase. Is it becoming easier to use or more complex? Do the people who maintain the technology actually care about the quality of their product? Have there recently been a lot of serious security vulnerabilities in the software that seem like they were the result of poor programming?

Other Reasons

There are other aspects to consider when you're choosing a technology—primarily its simplicity and how suitable it is for your purposes. Personal opinion can play a part, too, after you've taken into account all the practical considerations. Some people like the way one programming language *looks* better than the way another one does. That can sometimes be a valid reason to choose a technology—if you just like one technology more than another, and everything else is equal between them, go with the one that makes you happy. After all, you're the one who's going to be using it—your opinion matters! The guidelines above will help you weed out the definitely bad choices; the rest is up to your personal research, requirements, and desires.

Complexity and the Wrong Solution

Often, if something is getting very complex, that means there is an error in the design somewhere far below the level where the complexity appears.

For example, it's very difficult to make a car drive fast if it has square wheels. Tuning the engine isn't going to solve the problem—you need to redesign the car so that its wheels are round.

Any time there's an "unsolvable complexity" in your program, it's because there's something fundamentally wrong with the design. If the problem appears unsolvable at one level, back up and look at what might be underlying the problem.

Programmers actually do this quite often. You may find yourself saying, "I have this terribly messy code, and it's really complex to add a new feature!" Well, your fundamental problem there is that the code is messy. Clean it up, make the already existing code simple, and you'll find that adding the new feature will be simple as well.

What Problem Are You Trying to Solve?

If somebody comes up to you and says something like, "How do I make this pony fly to the moon?" the question you need to ask is, "What problem are you trying to solve?" You may find out that what this person really needs is to collect some gray rocks. Why he thought he had to fly to the moon, and use a *pony* to do it, only he may know. People do get confused like this. Ask them what *problem* they're trying to solve, though, and a simple solution will start to present itself. For example, in this case, once we understand the problem fully, the solution becomes simple and obvious: he should just walk outside and find some gray rocks—no pony required.

So, when things get complex, back up and take a look at the problem you're trying to solve. Take a *really big* step back. You are allowed to question *everything*. Maybe you thought that adding two and two was the only way to get four, and you didn't think about adding one and three instead, or skipping the addition entirely and just putting four there. The problem is, "How do I get the number four?" *Any* method of solving that problem is acceptable, so what you need to do is figure out what the best method would be for the situation that you're in.

Discard your assumptions. Really *look* at the problem you're trying to solve. Make sure that you fully understand every aspect of it, and then figure out the simplest way to solve it. Don't ask, "How do I solve this problem using my current code?" or "How did Professor Anne solve this problem in her program?" No—just ask yourself, "How, in general, in a perfect world, should this sort of problem be solved?" From there, you might see how your code needs to be reworked. Then you can rework your code. *Then* you can solve the problem.

Complex Problems

Sometimes you will be called upon to solve a problem that is inherently very complex —for example, spell checking, or making a computer play chess. This doesn't mean that your solution has to be complex, but it does mean that you will have to work harder than usual to simplify your code when dealing with this problem.

If you're having trouble with a complex problem, write it down on paper in plain language, or draw it out as a diagram. Some of the best programming is done on paper, really. Putting it into the computer is just a minor detail.

Many difficult design problems can be solved by simply drawing or writing them out on paper.

Handling Complexity

As a programmer, you will run into complexity. Other programmers will write complex programs that you will have to fix. Hardware designers and language designers will make your life difficult.

If some part of *your* system is too complex, there is a specific way to fix it—redesign the individual pieces, in small steps. Each fix should be as small as you can safely make it without introducing further complexity. When you're going through this process, the greatest danger is that you could possibly introduce *more* complexity with your fixes. This is why so many redesigns or rewrites ultimately fail—they introduce more complexity than they fix, or they end up being just as complex as the original system was.

Each step could be as small as giving a single variable a better name, or just adding a few comments to confusing code. But more often, the steps involve splitting one complex piece into multiple simple pieces.

For example, if you have one long file that contains all of your code, start improving it by splitting off *one* tiny piece into a separate file. Then improve the design of that tiny piece. Then split off some other tiny piece of the system into a new file, and improve its design. Continue like this, and eventually you'll end up with a reliable, understandable, and maintainable system.

If your system is *very* complex, this can take quite a bit of work, so you must be patient. You must first conceive of a system that is *simpler* than the one you have now—even if just in a small way. Then you work toward that simpler system, step by step. Once you reach that simpler system, you again conceive an even *simpler* system, and work toward that. You don't ever have to conceive the "perfect" system, because there is no such thing. You just have to continuously work toward a system that is *better* than the one you have now, and eventually you will reach a highly manageable level of simplicity.

It is important to note, however, that you cannot stop writing features and spend a long time just redesigning. The Law of Change tells us that the environment around your program will be continuously changing, and thus your program's functionality must adapt. If you fail to adapt and improve from the user's perspective for any significant length of time, you risk the loss of your user base and the death of your project.

There are, thankfully, various ways to balance these two needs of writing features and handling complexity. One of the best ways is to do your redesigning purely with the goal of making some specific feature easier to implement, and then implementing that feature. That way, you switch regularly between redesign work and feature work. This also helps your new design fit your needs well, because you're creating it with a real use in mind. Your system will slowly get less complex over time, and you will still keep pace with your users' needs. You can even do this for bugs—if you see that some bug would be easier to fix with a different design, redesign the code before fixing it.

Redesigning for a Feature

A project named Bugzilla stores all of its data in a database. Bugzilla only supports one particular database system for storing data, named OldDB. Some new customers want to use a different database system to store data, named NewDB. These customers have good reasons to want this feature: they understand NewDB much better than OldDB, and they already have NewDB running at their companies. But all the existing customers want to keep using OldDB.

So, Bugzilla has to start supporting more than one database. This will require a *lot* of code changes, as Bugzilla doesn't have any centralized code for storing and receiving information from the database. Instead, there are lots of custom database commands spread throughout the code that are specific to OldDB and won't work on NewDB.

One option is to sprinkle `if` statements throughout the entire codebase, writing different code for NewDB and OldDB everywhere that the database gets accessed. This would roughly double the complexity of the entire codebase, though, and the Bugzilla team consists of only a few part-time programmers. If the system's complexity doubled, they could no longer maintain it.

Instead, the Bugzilla team decides to redesign the system so that it can support multiple databases easily. This is a huge project. Here is a high-level overview of how they accomplish it:

1. There exist some standard database commands that work on *any* database system, but they aren't always being used. Go through the system and fix one file at a time, changing it to use standard commands where possible.

2. For the database commands where there is no standard version, create functions that will return the right command for the database in use. One function is created for one nonstandard command, and then every instance of that nonstandard command is replaced with the function call. Continue this process until all nonstandard functions are gone.

3. Numerous pieces of code are designed entirely around features that exist only in OldDB. Stop using those OldDB-specific features, and instead use standard features that will work on all database systems. Fix these features one at a time, in multiple steps if necessary.

4. Redesign Bugzilla's installation system so that it can set itself up on any database system, not just OldDB. This involves first redesigning the installation system to be simpler, and then adjusting that simple code to support both OldDB and NewDB.

Each step above is a project in and of itself. They are all broken down into smaller steps, so that good design can be done on each piece of work. Also, the system is tested after any change is made, to be sure that it still works the same way on OldDB as it did before.

Does this result in a perfect system? No. But it does result in a system that is *better* than it was before—in addition to supporting NewDB, the code is now much easier to maintain. Eventually Bugzilla expanded to support four different database systems, all because this work made it so much easier to support new ones.[2]

Making One Piece Simpler

The above is all well and good, but what do you actually *do* to make one piece simpler? Well, this is where all of the world's existing knowledge about software design comes into play. It helps a lot to study up on design patterns, methods of dealing with legacy code, and all the tools of software engineering in general. It can be particularly helpful to know multiple programming languages and be familiar with many different libraries, because each involves different ways of thinking about problems that could be applicable to your situation, even if you're not using those languages or libraries.

Studying those materials will give you many options to choose from when you are faced with a complexity. The laws of software design can help you pick which options are good, and then your judgment and experience can determine what to actually do with your specific problem. Never robotically apply a tool purely because some authority has deemed it best—always do what is right for the code you're looking at and the situation you're in.

Sometimes, though, you may look at a piece of code and not know *any* tools to use to simplify it. Or you may be new to programming and not have the time to study up on all this information immediately. In that case, you should just look at the complexity and ask yourself, "How could this be easier to deal with or more understandable?" That's the key question behind every simplification. *Any* true answer to it is a valid way of making your code simpler; the tools and techniques of software design just help us come up with *better* answers.

Unfixable Complexity

When you are working on simplifying your system, you may find that some complexity is hard to avoid, like the complexity of the underlying hardware. If you run into an unfixable complexity like this, your goal is to *hide* the complexity. Put a wrapper around it that is simple for other programmers to use and understand.

---

2. Bugzilla was redesigned in this fashion many times, over many years, for many different reasons. If you'd like to see a history of the major work that was done, you can look at the crossed-out items here: *https://bugzilla.mozilla.org/showdependencytree.cgi?id=278579&hide_resolved=0*. If you'd just like more specifics about how the database work was done, see the crossed-out items here: *https://bugzilla.mozilla.org/showdependencytree.cgi?id=98304&hide_resolved=0*. Reading the title of each item should give you an idea of how the project was accomplished, if you're familiar with database systems.

Rewriting

Some designers, when faced with a very complex system, throw it out and start over again. However, rewriting a system from the ground up is essentially an admission of failure as a designer. It is making the statement, "We failed to design a maintainable system and so must start over."

Some people believe that *all* systems must eventually be rewritten. This is not true. It *is* possible to design a system that never needs to be thrown away. A software designer saying "We'll have to throw the whole thing away someday anyway" would be much like a building architect saying "This skyscraper will fall down someday anyway." If the skyscraper were poorly designed and not maintained well, then yes, someday it would fall down. But if it were built right to start with and then properly maintained, why would it collapse?

It is just as possible to build maintainable software systems as it is to build sound skyscrapers.

Now, with all that said, there are situations in which rewriting is acceptable. However, they are very rare. You should only rewrite if *all* of the following are true:

1. You have developed an accurate estimate that shows that rewriting the system will be a more efficient use of time than redesigning the existing system. Don't just guess—do actual experiments with redesigning the existing system to see how it goes. It can be very hard to confront the existing complexity and resolve some piece of it, but you must actually attempt this a few times before you can know how much effort fixing all of it will require.

2. You have a tremendous amount of time to spend on creating a new system.

3. You are somehow a better designer than the original designer of the system or, if you *are* the original designer, your design skills have improved drastically since you designed the original system.

4. You fully intend to design this new system in a series of simple steps and have users who can give you feedback for each step along the way.

5. You have the resources available to both maintain the existing system and design a new system at the same time. *Never* stop maintaining a system that is currently in use so that the programmers can rewrite it. Systems must *always* be maintained if they are in use. And remember that your personal attention is also a resource"that must be taken into account here—do you have enough time available in each day to be a designer on both the new system and the old system simultaneously, if you are going to work on both?

If all of the above points are true, you may be in a situation where it is acceptable to rewrite. Otherwise, the correct thing to do is to handle the complexity of the existing system *without* a rewrite, by improving the system's design in a series of simple steps.

CHAPTER 8

Testing

There is no certainty that a program will run in the future—there is only the certainty that a program is running now. Even if you've run it once, it may not run again. Perhaps the environment will change around it so it will no longer function. Perhaps you'll run it on a different computer, and it won't work on the new machine.

However, there is hope—we are not doomed to endless uncertainty about the functionality of our software. The Law of Testing tells us the way out:

The degree to which you know how your software behaves is the degree to which you have accurately tested it.[1]

The more recently you've tested your software, the more likely it is that it still works. The more environments you've tested it in, the more certain you can be that it works in those circumstances. This is part of what we mean when we talk about the "degree" of testing—how many aspects of the software you've tested, how recently, and in how many different environments. In general, you could simply say:

Unless you've tried it, you don't know that it works.

Saying "it works" is actually quite vague, though—what do you mean by "works"? What you really know when you test is that your software *behaves as you intended it to*. Thus, you have to know what behavior you intended. That may sound stupid and obvious, but it's a critical fact in testing. You must ask a very precise question with every test, and get a very specific answer. The question could be something like, "What happens when a user presses this button as the first thing he does after the application starts, when the application has never been started before?" And you should be looking for some specific answer, such as, "The application displays a window that says 'Hello, World!'"

So, you have a question, and you know what the answer should be. If you get some other answer, then your software is "not working."

---

1. This law is considerably newer than the others and I would welcome any verification or counter-examples that you have for it.

Sometimes a behavior is very hard to test, and you can only ask, "If a user does this, does the program crash?" and expect the answer, "No." But with well-designed software, in most situations, you can get much more specific information than that with your tests.

And of course, you must also make your tests *accurate*. If they tell you that the program is behaving properly when it is not—or tell you that it's broken when it's actually working fine—they are inaccurate tests.

Finally, you must observe the results of your tests in order for them to be valid. If they fail, there must be some way for you to know that they failed, and specifically *how* they failed.

Testing can be easy to overlook. We write some code, save it, and forget to ever see if it actually *works*. But no matter how brilliant a programmer you are, no matter how many mathematical proofs you do to show that your code is correct, you don't know that it works unless you've actually tried to use it.

And if at any point you change a piece of your software, you no longer know that that piece works. It must be tested again. Furthermore, that piece is likely connected to lots of other pieces, so you now don't know if any of *those* pieces work, either. If your change is big enough, you may have to test the whole program again.

Obviously, you don't want to have to manually test your whole program every time you make a tiny change. So, in modern times, developers usually apply this law by creating automated tests for every piece of code that they write. The nice thing about that is that they can just run the tests right after they make any change, and those automated tests will test every single piece of the system to make sure *everything* still works after each individual change.

There is a lot of information on the Internet and in books about writing automated tests and about testing in general—it's a very well covered area, and it's worth reading up on. The Law of Testing just explains why we should test, when we should test, and what information tests are actually giving us.

The Laws of Software Design

This appendix summarizes all of the actual laws discussed in this book:

1. The purpose of software is *to help people.*
2. The Equation of Software Design:

$$D = \frac{V_n + V_f}{E_i + E_m}$$

   where:

   D
   > Stands for the *desirability* of the change.

   V_n
   > Stands for *value now.*

   V_f
   > Stands for *future value.*

   E_i
   > Stands for the *effort of implementation.*

   E_m
   > Stands for the *effort of maintenance.*

   This is the primary law of software design. As time goes on, this equation reduces to:

$$D = \frac{V_f}{E_m}$$

   Which demonstrates that *it is more important to reduce the effort of maintenance than it is to reduce the effort of implementation.*

3. The Law of Change: The longer your program exists, the more probable it is that any piece of it will have to change.

4. The Law of Defect Probability: The chance of introducing a defect into your program is proportional to the size of the changes you make to it.

5. The Law of Simplicity: The ease of maintenance of any piece of software is proportional to the simplicity of its individual pieces.

6. The Law of Testing: The degree to which you know how your software behaves is the degree to which you have accurately tested it.

That's it. Many more facts and ideas were discussed in this book, but these six items are the *laws* of software design. Note that of all of these, the most important to bear in mind are the purpose of software, the reduced form of the Equation of Software Design, and the Law of Simplicity.

If you wanted to sum up the most important facts to keep in mind about software design in two simple sentences, they would be:

- It is more important to reduce the effort of maintenance than it is to reduce the effort of implementation.
- The effort of maintenance is proportional to the complexity of the system.

Armed with only those two statements and an understanding of the purpose of software, you could very possibly re-evolve everything in this book, provided that you also understood that the complexity of the system actually comes from the complexity of its individual pieces.

Facts, Laws, Rules, and Definitions

This appendix lists every single major fact, law, rule, and definition covered in this book:

- *Fact*: The difference between a bad programmer and a good programmer is *understanding*. That is, bad programmers don't understand what they are doing, and good programmers do.
- *Rule*: A good programmer should do everything in his power to make what he writes simple for other programmers to use and comprehend.
- *Fact*: Everybody who writes software is a designer.
- *Rule:* Design is not a democracy. Decisions should be made by individuals.
- **Law**: The purpose of software is *to help people*.

- **Law**: The Equation of Software Design:

$$D = \frac{V_n + V_f}{E_i + E_m}$$

This is the Primary Law of Software Design. Or, in English:

The desirability of a change is directly proportional to the value now plus the future value, and inversely proportional to the effort of implementation plus the effort of maintenance.

As time goes on, this equation reduces to:

$$D = \frac{V_f}{E_m}$$

Which demonstrates that it is more important to reduce the effort of maintenance than it is to reduce the effort of implementation.

- *Rule*: The quality level of your design should be proportional to the length of future time in which your system will continue to help people.
- *Rule*: There are some things about the future that you do not know.
- *Fact*: The most common and disastrous error that programmers make is predicting something about the future when in fact they cannot know.
- *Rule*: You are safest if you don't attempt to predict the future at all, and instead make all your design decisions based on immediately known present-time information.
- **Law**: The Law of Change: The longer your program exists, the more probable it is that any piece of it will have to change.
- *Fact*: The three mistakes (called "the three flaws" in this book) that software designers are prone to making in coping with the Law of Change are:
  1. Writing code that isn't needed
  2. Not making the code easy to change
  3. Being too generic
- *Rule*: Don't write code until you actually need it, and remove any code that isn't being used.
- *Rule*: Code should be designed based on what you know now, not on what you think will happen in the future.
- *Fact*: When your design actually makes things more complex instead of simplifying things, you're overengineering.
- *Rule*: Be only as generic as you know you need to be right now.
- *Rule*: You can avoid the three flaws by doing incremental development and design.
- **Law**: The Law of Defect Probability: The chance of introducing a defect into your program is proportional to the size of the changes you make to it.
- *Rule*: The best design is the one that allows for the most change in the environment with the least change in the software.
- *Rule*: Never "fix" anything unless it's a problem, and you have evidence showing that the problem really exists.
- *Rule*: In any particular system, any piece of information should, ideally, exist only once.
- **Law**: The Law of Simplicity: The ease of maintenance of any piece of software is proportional to the simplicity of its individual pieces.
- *Fact*: Simplicity is relative.
- *Rule*: If you really want to succeed, it is best to be stupid, dumb simple.
- *Rule*: Be consistent.
- *Rule*: Readability of code depends primarily on how space is occupied by letters and symbols.

- *Rule*: Names should be long enough to fully communicate what something is or does without being so long that they become hard to read.
- *Rule*: Comments should explain *why* the code is doing something, not *what* it is doing.
- *Rule*: Simplicity requires design.
- *Rule*: You can create complexity by:
    — Expanding the purpose of your software
    — Adding programmers to the team
    — Changing things that don't need to be changed
    — Being locked into bad technologies
    — Misunderstanding
    — Poor design or no design
    — Reinventing the wheel
    — Violating the purpose of your software
- *Rule*: You can determine whether or not a technology is "bad" by looking at its survival potential, interoperability, and attention to quality.
- *Rule*: Often, if something is getting very complex, that means there is an error in the design somewhere below the level where the complexity appears.
- *Rule*: When presented with complexity, ask, "What problem are you trying to solve?"
- *Rule*: Many difficult design problems can be solved by simply drawing or writing them out on paper.
- *Rule*: To handle complexity in your system, redesign the individual pieces in small steps.
- *Fact*: The key question behind all valid simplifications is, "How could this be easier to deal with or more understandable?"
- *Rule*: If you run into an unfixable complexity outside of your program, put a wrapper around it that is simple for other programmers.
- *Rule*: Rewriting is acceptable only in a very limited set of situations.
- **Law**: The Law of Testing: The degree to which you know how your software behaves is the degree to which you have accurately tested it.
- *Rule:* Unless you've tried it, you don't know that it works.

About the Author

Max Kanat-Alexander, Chief Architect of the open-source Bugzilla Project, Google Software Engineer, and writer, has been fixing computers since he was eight years old and writing software since he was fourteen. He is the author of http://www.codesimplicity.com/ and http://www.fedorafaq.org, and is currently living in Northern California.

Get even more for your money.

Join the O'Reilly Community, and register the O'Reilly books you own. It's free, and you'll get:

- $4.99 ebook upgrade offer
- 40% upgrade offer on O'Reilly print books
- Membership discounts on books and events
- Free lifetime updates to ebooks and videos
- Multiple ebook formats, DRM FREE
- Participation in the O'Reilly community
- Newsletters
- Account management
- 100% Satisfaction Guarantee

Signing up is easy:

1. **Go to: oreilly.com/go/register**
2. **Create an O'Reilly login.**
3. **Provide your address.**
4. **Register your books.**

Note: English-language books only

To order books online:
oreilly.com/store

For questions about products or an order:
orders@oreilly.com

To sign up to get topic-specific email announcements and/or news about upcoming books, conferences, special offers, and new technologies:
elists@oreilly.com

For technical questions about book content:
booktech@oreilly.com

To submit new book proposals to our editors:
proposals@oreilly.com

O'Reilly books are available in multiple DRM-free ebook formats. For more information:
oreilly.com/ebooks

O'REILLY®

Spreading the knowledge of innovators   oreilly.com

Have it your way.

O'Reilly eBooks

- Lifetime access to the book when you buy through oreilly.com
- Provided in up to four DRM-free file formats, for use on the devices of your choice: PDF, .epub, Kindle-compatible .mobi, and Android .apk
- Fully searchable, with copy-and-paste and print functionality
- Alerts when files are updated with corrections and additions

oreilly.com/ebooks/

Safari Books Online

- Access the contents and quickly search over 7000 books on technology, business, and certification guides
- Learn from expert video tutorials, and explore thousands of hours of video on technology and design topics
- Download whole books or chapters in PDF format, at no extra cost, to print or read on the go
- Get early access to books as they're being written
- Interact directly with authors of upcoming books
- Save up to 35% on O'Reilly print books

See the complete Safari Library at safari.oreilly.com